In the
COMPANY
of MEN

First Simon Pulse edition September 2002

Text copyright © 2001 by Nancy Mace

"As the Cadets Go Rolling Along," page 140, extracted from the Guidon. 2000-2001

"The Cadet Prayer," pages 157-158, by Bishop S. Thomas, Ret. First Honor Graduate

Class of 1892

Simon Pulse

An imprint of Simon & Schuster

Children's Publishing Division

1230 Avenue of the Americas

New York, NY 10020

Also available in a Simon & Schuster Books for Young Readers hardcover edition.

Book design by Paula Winicur

The text of this book was set in Bembo.

Printed in the United States of America

2 4 6 8 10 9 7 5 3 1

The Library of Congress has cataloged the hardcover edition as follows:

In the company of men/by Nancy Mace; with Mary Jane Ross.—1st ed.

p. cm.

ISBN: 978-0-689-84003-6

1. Mace, Nancy—Juvenile literature. 2. Women military cadets—South Carolina—Biography—
Juvenile literature. 3. Citadel, the Military College of South Carolina—Biography—Juvenile lit-
erature [1.Mace, Nancy. 2. Military cadets. 3. Citadel, the Military College of South Carolina—
Biography. 4. Women—Biography.] 1. Ross, Mary Jane. 11. Title.

U53.M255A3 2001

355'.0071'173—dc21   2001020544

ISBN 0-689-84003-9 (Simon Pulse pbk.)

★ DEDICATION ★

To my mother for her strength, courage,

and support to withstand all storms;

and to my father who taught me that hard work

and determination can overcome any challenge,

but also for never letting me forget my sense of humor in the process.

★ CONTENTS ★

PREFACE

If you visit The Citadel museum today, you will find a picture of me. It is mounted in a glass case near the end of the exhibits, adjacent to a photo of the first African-American to graduate from the Corps. The explanatory note next to my predecessor's name, written by a Citadel patron, lists the cadet's accomplishments and ends with warm comments on the value of his achievement. In a college originally founded to protect the citizenry from insurgent slaves, this young man's success is pointed out as the hallmark of a new era for the long gray line. My photo, displayed a few inches below his, is also accompanied by explanatory comments. The text notes that I am the first female graduate of The Citadel, then follows with a factual list of my awards and achievements during my three years in the Corps. And that is all. The appreciative commentary that characterizes my groundbreaking predecessor is conspicuously absent. The silence speaks volumes.

I am not surprised. In a city that values tradition above all, I represent change, and change never comes easily to Charleston, South Carolina. What the keepers of The Citadel flame fail to realize is that I did not come to the college to destroy its tradition. I came to fulfill it.

I am deeply proud of the values my college reveres: courage, honor, and reverence for the past. Those are the values of the "Citadel Man," the values I have always seen in my father, The Citadel's most decorated living graduate. I followed in my father's footsteps because I wanted to embrace my family's past, and because I wanted to point the way to the future. I sought to demonstrate that the values the college holds most dear have nothing to do with gender. Faced with the same challenges, given the same opportunity, women can be as courageous, honorable, and reverent as any man. I tried to do my part in demonstrating that.

I did not do it alone. A host of faculty, administrators, alumni, classmates, and total strangers poured out their hearts and their wisdom to help me succeed. I am deeply indebted to them, for I would not be writing this book today without their support during my journey. The first lesson of freshman year is that only team players survive in the Corps, that no one can do it alone. I lived that lesson. During my first week as a knob, I could not imagine surviving freshman year. When the second year started and life got even harder, I never thought I would see graduation. And when graduation day came at last, I stood by the edge of the stage, pale as a ghost, wondering how I had gotten there. I got there with the help of my friends.

Critics speculate whether I could have gotten there without my father. Such speculation bespeaks not only an ignorance of The Citadel, but an ignorance of my father. My father became Commandant of the Corps midway through my second semester there. Like every Commandant's child before me, I immediately became the focus of intensified harassment and suspicion that had little to do with my gender. My father's only hesitation in accepting the position had been his concern for me, for he knew what the ramifications would be. We both did. Once he became Commandant, I ceased to be his daughter while on campus. In his eyes, I was just another cadet, and the one time I walked into his office without an appointment, he threw me out in wrath. In spite of the personal repercussions for me, however, I have never regretted my father's decision. The Citadel is a far less menacing and far more disciplined place because he came there. I could not be prouder of the changes he has made.

Journalists have repeatedly asked me how it feels to be a pioneer. I wouldn't know. I do not think of myself as a pioneer; I think of myself as a cadet, like the thousands of male cadets who preceded me—and the thousands of female and male cadets who will follow me. I am proud to be numbered among them.

BRIEF HISTORY OF THE CITADEL

Located on the Ashley River in Charleston, South Carolina, The Citadel embodies the fierce pride and deep sense of tradition that characterize this historic region.

The college was founded in 1842 as part of the original South Carolina Military Academy. Its dual purpose was to offer a free education to deserving young men and to provide a well-trained militia for the protection of Charleston. From the beginning, The Citadel has played a part in American military history that far outweighs its size. Citadel cadets fired the first shots of the War Between the States against the federal ship *Star of the West* in January 1861, and four months later they took part in the historic bombardment of Fort Sumter. Cadets took part in every major battle of the War, and it was a Citadel cadet who carried the flag of truce to General Custer at Appomatox Court House.

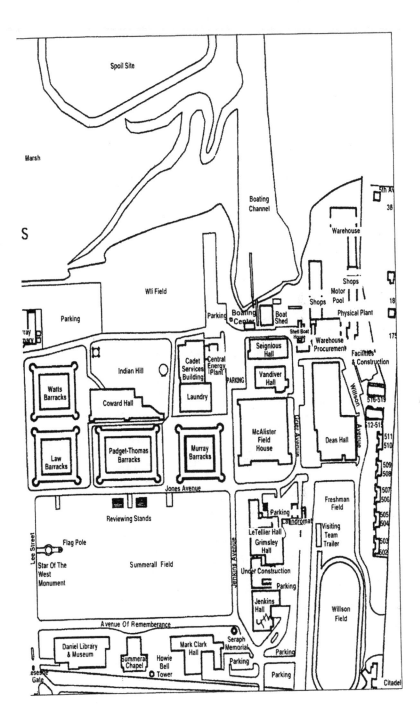

PROLOGUE: REMEMBRANCE

The room was small and white, filled with battered tan metal furniture. To my right was a double rack with two thin mattresses and a wool blanket, Citadel blue. The room smelled of shoe polish, mildew, and tobacco spit.

I stood rigidly at attention, chin pressed against my throat, eyes straight ahead, forehead fixed in a frown. My uniform clung stickily to my body, damp in the muggy Charleston air. A few feet away, a muscular young man in a gray uniform was pacing up and down. We were the only two people in the room.

Finally, he stopped in front of me, put his face a few inches from mine, stared intently into my eyes, and began to speak. I could feel his hot breath on my throat.

"Mace, I know why you are here. I know all about your past. I have heard the rumors. I know why you came."

My throat constricted, and the familiar anger welled up inside. "Asshole!" I muttered in my head. "What a jerk!"

Then, leaning even closer, he considered me seriously for another moment and said, "I respect your decision to come here. I know what you're trying to do. I understand."

He started to say something else, thought better of it, and finally dismissed me to return to my quarters. As I saluted him and stepped out into the sultry evening air, I looked up at the white galleries towering above me. Tears of rage stung my eyes. "The hell you know why I'm here," I thought. "The hell you do. Nobody knows. Nobody but me."

★ CHAPTER 1 ★

BATTLE CRY

I am a general's daughter. I know a battle when I see one. I never dreamed, however, that the battle to graduate a woman from The Citadel would turn out to be mine.

Looking back on it now, my coming to The Citadel seems like destiny. I grew up in the home of The Citadel's most decorated living graduate, Brigadier General Emory Mace. My father grew up "poor but proud," to use the local phrase. Dad was very young when my grandfather died, so from an early age my father and grandmother struggled to make ends meet in the low country of South Carolina. There were few jobs for women in those days, but my grandmother found work with the county office of children's social services. The pay was low, but she believed strongly in community service and found satisfaction in her work. My father did his part, taking odd jobs to help his mother while he was still a young boy. And like so many low country boys, he became a skilled hunter and fisherman. The woods around South Carolina provided him both with adventure and with fish and game for his mother to cook for dinner. When he was big enough, he also began to catch alligators in the local marshes and sell them for profit. It wasn't strictly legal, but it brought in much-needed money, and the neighbors pretty much looked the other way. If Dad could help his family get by, all the better.

My dad has always said that it was The Citadel that changed his life. Among his other jobs, Dad drove the local school bus during high school to make ends meet. It was through this job that he met a Citadel graduate who took a liking to my father and wanted to help him. Recognizing my father's grit and intelligence, he offered to sponsor Dad for admission to The Citadel. At the time, my father knew almost nothing about the College. He did know, however, that college would give him an education and a chance in life he would otherwise never have. Dad accepted the man's offer gratefully, and arrangements were made for my father to become a cadet. The afternoon that a relative dropped Dad off at Padgett–Thomas Barracks, near the center of campus, my father's life changed forever.

From the time I was a little girl, I heard stories of my father's college days. His scholarship and loans didn't begin to cover all his expenses, so to make up the deficit, my dad would go into the swamps near the Ashley River at night and poach alligators like he had as a boy. It was a dangerous but profitable business that paid his tuition for four years. Dad soon became famous on campus for his backwoods stunts. There is a picture in the 1963 Citadel yearbook that shows him posing with a live alligator. Dad is standing on the second gallery of 2nd Battalion, holding the alligator by the neck. The animal's tail dangles down to my dad's feet, and its jaws are wide open, just inches from my father's face, as it struggles to get loose. Another time Dad sank a metal spike in the grass on Summerall Field and chained a large alligator to it in the dark of night. The next morning he watched through his barracks window and chuckled as frightened senior officers tried to remove the alligator from the field. Everyone knew who had done it, but no one could prove it, and Dad escaped punishment.

Once he became an upperclassman, my father quickly became a legend among the "knobs" (freshmen) assigned to him. Every knob in his company looked at my father with a combination of hatred and awe. When he got a craving for roast duck, Dad would go hunting and make his knobs pluck and clean the birds for him, then take the ducks to the Mess Hall for roasting. A college photo shows a line-up of unhappy freshmen holding a brace of dead ducks ripe for plucking. The most famous knob incident, however, took place during my father's senior year. My dad didn't think one of his knobs was toeing the line, so when Dad returned from a poaching expedition before dawn one morning, he opened his knob's door and threw the angry alligator into the room where the unsuspecting freshman was sleeping. Dad watched just long enough to see the terrified cadet scramble to the top bunk with his roommate, then shut the door and walked away. He eventually went back and retrieved the angry alligator, but he had made his point. Nobody messed with my dad.

My father is the product of another time and place, and many people don't understand him. They see only his toughness, but I have always seen his courage. The walls of our house were lined with medals for bravery in battle, and I knew my dad had risked his life over and over again to save his men in battle. For as long as I can remember, my father has been my hero. I wanted nothing more than to prove that I was my father's daughter, to make him proud of me. I had little hope that would ever happen.

Life had always been a battle for me. I was a skinny, sensitive little girl, prone to sickness and often unhappy. My father was gone much of the time and paid little attention to me when he was home. I sometimes wondered if he even loved me. My mother was my primary source of comfort and strength, in part because we are so much alike. I always knew she loved me; I also knew there were times when she could have killed me. Looking back on my early years, Mom says she didn't always know whether to hug me or strangle me. I wasn't an easy child to raise, and I often taxed her patience to the limit.

School was difficult for me from the beginning. My mother vividly remembers the struggle of sending me off to kindergarten. I was deeply attached to my younger brother, James, fiercely protective, and convinced that it was my job to take care of him. When I first learned that I would not be taking James to school with me, I fell apart. It took all my mother's patient reassurance to convince me that I should leave James in her hands. From my first day of kindergarten, she had trouble getting me to leave the house. Part of the problem was that I worried constantly about getting everything just right. Dressed for school each morning in my little dresses and fold-down socks, I would be fussing with my socks before I even finished breakfast. For reasons my mother could not understand, I was convinced that I couldn't leave the house unless my socks were folded exactly even. Every morning she would have to get out the ruler and measure my socks, carefully adjusting the folds until they were exactly even. When she finally lost patience and tried to make me leave the house without the usual ritual, I burst into tears and cried as if my heart would break. Torn between worry and exasperation, Mom got the ruler out and adjusted my socks until I stopped crying. She tells me that she was never sure whether I was worried that the people at school wouldn't like me if I wasn't perfect, or whether I was simply finding reasons not to leave her. Probably a little of both. Fortunately, my mother is a combination of strength, compassion, and patience, for I required all three.

Fortunately, I did have my father's persistence—my mother would say stubbornness—and that persistence eventually paid off. When I was six years old, my mother took me to a swim meet to watch my older sister, Mary, compete. Thrilled at the sight of my sister racing through the water, I announced at dinner that night that I wanted to join the swim team, too. At the time, I was small for my age and could barely flounder the few yards across the shallow end of a pool. My mother diplomatically informed me that summer was over, my swimsuit was already packed in a box at the top of the closet, and it was too late to join my sister's team. Thinking that would be the end of the discussion, she put me to bed and forgot about it.

Hours later, long after she and my father had gone to sleep, she was awakened by a noise in the next room. Tracing the noise to my bedroom, she found me balanced on the top of a chair in the closet, boxes tumbled around my feet. I was triumphantly holding my swimsuit. I announced that I was now "all ready" to join the swim team. It was two o'clock in the morning. Too tired to argue, my mother promised to take me to the pool after school the next day and tucked me back into bed. Mom kept her promise, and the following afternoon she somehow convinced the team coach to take on an undersized girl who could barely swim. At my first meet, I struggled to reach the end of the pool long after the other girls had finished the race and dried off. Any other child would have given up, but not me. Meet after meet, I splashed awkwardly down the length of the pool, and by the end of the season I was keeping up with the slower, older swimmers. The following year I began winning, eventually becoming a champion swimmer. I had learned my first lesson in persistence.

About the same time I first jumped into the deep end of a pool, our family received a visit from an old college friend of my dad's named Jimmy Jones. My father had given me a blue Citadel T-shirt from the College gift shop and taught me how to brace and salute like a cadet. When I heard that the visiting friend was from The Citadel, I insisted on wearing my shirt and greeting him with a salute when he pulled up to the house in his car. An old family photograph shows me standing at attention, my chin tucked in, my face serious with concentration as I salute Mr. Jones. My mother captured the moment on film and tucked the snapshot away in an album for more than a decade. It would be twelve years before any of us thought of that picture again.

Life didn't get any easier for me with the passing of the years. I didn't know it yet, but I was suffering the increasing effects of a learning disability called attention deficit disorder. Academics had always been a source of frustration and shame for me. I had trouble focusing or memorizing, my thought processes were often disrupted, and long periods of forced concentration made me want to crawl out of my skin. The increasing demands of my high school curriculum were rapidly becoming too much for me. It was humiliating. There were days I just wanted to give up.

I didn't seem to fit in socially, either. As an Army brat, I moved constantly with my family, so it was difficult to form lasting friendships. By the time I entered my teens, I was deeply confused about who I was and where I belonged. No matter where I turned, I felt like an outsider. I tried to fit in by partying my freshman year of high school, but it only made things worse. By my sophomore year, I was so miserable that my parents sent me to Florida, to stay with my older sister, Beth Ann, for a while. For several months, I baby-sat my nieces and nephews and worked as a lifeguard at the local beach, entering several lifeguarding competitions as well. When summer ended, I returned to my parents' house and my old high school, hoping that this time things would go better there. Instead, everything just got worse.

Because I had been gone for several months, gossip began to circulate that I'd been pregnant and gone away to have the baby. The rumors grew and grew, and some of the guys at school started treating me like the town slut. I began getting nasty prank calls at home, and when I walked down the hallways at school, some of the football players would purposely bump into me or press me up against the walls and make lewd comments. My mother changed our phone number and bought caller ID, but there was no way to stop people's tongues. Soon other rumors followed: I was a drug addict, I'd had an abortion for a second pregnancy, and on and on. It never seemed to stop. Worst of all, nobody even seemed to care if what they said was true. They liked to gossip too much to let the truth get in the way. The final blow came during junior year, when a good friend of mine was killed by a drunk driver the day after a party I had attended. I was devastated. I sank into a depression so deep that I required antidepressants just to get through the days. I had hit rock bottom. I no longer cared whether I lived or died, and that terrified me. I needed help.

My mother, worried about me, took me out of school and forced me to go through a series of psychological and neurological tests. The tests revealed what my mom already suspected: that I had ADD, a neurological condition that made it difficult for me to learn. At first I resisted the diagnosis, for I didn't like to be labeled "learning disabled." Eventually, though, with my mother's help, I began to accept the reality of my condition. I started on prescription medication for the ADD and worked to acquire coping skills to help me compensate for my disability. The seeds of hope began to grow within me, and with hope came renewed courage. I stopped taking the antidepressants and concentrated on other ways to get well.

Meanwhile, my mother arranged to have me home schooled by a friend of hers, a local teacher. Slowly, with Mom's support, I began to construct a happier life for myself. By the time I turned seventeen, I discovered to my astonishment that my grades had soared. Enrolling the following year in classes at Trident Tech, the local community college, my self-esteem was further boosted, as I found out that even there, I could compete—and frequently excel. For the first time in my life, I had hope that I might have a future after all. The same perseverance that had taken me the length of the pool when I was six was now helping me reach a more important goal—a happy and productive life.

It was about this same time that I started hearing about The Citadel once more, this time on the evening news. A high school girl named

Shannon Faulkner had accidentally been accepted to the all-male college, and all of South Carolina was in an uproar over it. Posters and bumper stickers began popping up all over the county, with SAVE THE MALES and 1800 BULLDOGS AND ONE BITCH pasted on the back of every pickup truck in town. An old friend of ours, now a member of the Board of Visitors, had a SAVE THE MALES sticker glued to the back of his Mercedes. Like most Southerners of their generation, my parents also opposed admitting a woman to The Citadel, not out of prejudice against women, but because they believed in the benefits of single-gender education. Always the achiever, my sister Mary had graduated from West Point by then, and my parents had supported her decision. Still, they believed that there should be places where a young man or woman could get an education without the distractions of the opposite sex.

I respected my parents' beliefs. It never once crossed my mind during high school to defy the rules and try to get admitted to my dad's college. It would have been disrespectful to my father.

In the early days of 1996, however, everything changed. Since The Citadel, like the Virginia Military Institute, is a state school supported by tax money, it has no choice but to follow the laws governing other public schools. Once the courts ruled that VMI had to admit women, it was clear that The Citadel would soon be forced to do the same. Preferring to take the step voluntarily, the College Board of Visitors voted in late June to admit women to the Corps of Cadets for the fall semester. Our old family friend Jimmy Jones, now head of the Board of Visitors, made the announcement on the evening news.

I guess you could say that was when fate intervened. As I watched the news that night, a thousand things went through my mind. I had put my life together for the first time, but I didn't know what to do next. I didn't want to attend West Point like my sister. What, then? Suddenly, here was my answer. I could follow in my father's steps, become a cadet like he was, stand where he stood. This was my chance to prove to my father, to the kids in high school who had laughed at me—to myself— that I had what it took. I could make something of myself. I could earn the respect that had eluded me for so long. After all, if I could survive as a woman at The Citadel, I could survive anything. I lay awake half the night, and by sunup, I knew what I had to do.

The next morning I drove down to the "Castle on the Ashley River," as I had dubbed the College, and filled out the necessary paperwork. I didn't say a word to anyone, not even my parents. On the following Monday the Admissions Department called to tell me to go ahead and get a physical and that so far, my application looked good. A few more days, and they would be able to give me a provisional answer.

Some secrets are just too big to keep, and I couldn't keep this one another minute. Brimming with excitement and anxiety, I was about to give my parents the surprise of their lives.

As with most of my secrets, I told my mother first. To say the least, she was surprised. It had never occurred to her that "her little girl" would be one of the first to apply to the Corps, and her first reaction was worry. She and I had been through a lot together the previous two years. And she still remembered the little girl who cried every day of kindergarten. We had a long talk about my reasons for applying. Finally, satisfied that I had thought my decision through carefully, she told me that if I really wanted to do this, she would be behind me 100 percent.

She made only one request: "Tell your father." I promised I would.

Telling Dad was harder, and it took me a few days to work up the courage. But I couldn't put off the conversation forever, so a week after I told my mother, I had a long talk with my dad. I began the conversation by telling him that I respected his viewpoint, and I knew he was against admitting women to his old college. As long as The Citadel opposed the entrance of women, I told him, I would never have applied there. But things had changed, and since the College was going to admit women anyway, I wanted to be one of them. I told him that I meant no disrespect to him. In fact, the main reason I had applied to the Corps of Cadets was because of him. I could think of no greater honor than to wear the uniform he had worn. I would work very hard to make him proud, I told him. Eventually, I ran out of words, and there was nothing to do but wait nervously for his reply.

My father is a master of the poker face, so it took a few moments to gauge his reaction. He sat there quietly, his unlit cigar clenched between his teeth, his jowls unmoving, his eyes noncommittal. At last he asked me the same question my mother had asked me: "Are you sure you know what you're getting into?"

I assured him, "Yes, sir, I think I do."

Unfortunately, he didn't think I had any real idea what I was getting myself into. I had to listen to an endless list of reasons why I shouldn't go to The Citadel. That evening, and for many weeks afterward, my father tried to discourage me from joining the Corps. I'm not sure he thought any woman could survive his old school. After all, most men couldn't. Still, there was a glint in his eye sometimes when he talked to me about his old school that told me he was proud of me for trying.

After all the bad publicity about women at The Citadel, I tried to keep my decision within the family as long as possible. That proved impossible. For starters, my dad "happened to mention" to our old Army friends that I would be entering The Citadel in the fall. Then, before I had even told my own friends, the evening news announced my decision to the whole world.

A New York attorney who was representing another female applicant somehow found out about my application and "accidentally" announced my name and hometown in open court. Within hours my name was on the Associated Press wires, and all hell broke loose.

All the major networks began calling our house. The caller ID on our home phone showed calls from ABC, NBC, CBS, and a host of local stations.

Meanwhile, the phone was also ringing off the hook with calls from relatives and family friends. "Did you know that they mentioned Nancy on the evening news tonight? So is it true? Is she really going to The Citadel?" All of them were astonished by the announcement, but most were supportive. Usually the questions were followed by "Well, good for her. Wish her luck for me, won't you?"

I was surprised and touched by the swell of support I began to receive. My parents and I were flooded with supportive calls, letters, and visits from family friends. Many of them were Army officers or Citadel alums, which felt especially good. I even received congratulations from a local judge, the Honorable Perry Murray. He made a point of seeking me out and saying, "Young lady, I want to shake your hand and congratulate you on your decision." Letters of encouragement began to pour in from all over the country as well, most simply addressed to

NANCY MACE, GOOSE CREEK, SOUTH CAROLINA. I was overwhelmed by the kindness of these strangers. After all the years of loneliness, I suddenly found myself surrounded by support. I was determined not to let any of these people down.

Soon articles about me started coming out in the papers, which was really strange. I wasn't used to seeing my name in print, but I kind of liked it. My favorite piece was an interview with General Fields, who was being evaluated for a position at The Citadel. In the course of an interview with a Charleston reporter, the general was asked for his views on women entering the Corps. The reporter mentioned my name as one of the women who would be attending. What the reporter didn't know was that General Fields was an old friend of my family who had lived across the street from us at Fort Richardson, Alaska, when I was growing up. The general told the reporter that he knew me personally, that he'd even been fishing with me and my dad. Then he said, "I wouldn't worry about Nancy. She'll do fine. She's as tough as woodpecker lips!" I thought it was hilarious.

A couple of weeks later, another funny incident happened at work. One afternoon the phone rang, and when I picked up the receiver and said, "This is Nancy Mace. May I help you?", the caller replied in surprise, "Really? *The* Nancy Mace? The famous one?"

Blushing and laughing, I replied, "I don't know about the famous part, but yes, this is Nancy Mace."

He laughed, too, and said, "Well, congratulations. And good luck!" I thought to myself as I transferred his call, "It's kind of cool being famous!" In the past, most of the attention I'd attracted was negative. For the first time, people were saying nice things about me.

Being famous wasn't always "cool," though, either for me or for my family. A few days later, my mother received her first piece of hate mail. The letter was handwritten and unsigned. The wording and tone were vicious and vaguely threatening, and I was hurt and angry. How dare this woman attack my mother that way? What kind of person had nothing better to do than write horrible letters to strangers? And what kind of coward sent a letter like that without signing her name? Unfortunately, that letter was only the first of many. The same woman wrote to my mother for nearly three years, all in the same threatening tone. My mother didn't tell me until much later, but there were times she feared for my safety.

Hate mail was the least of my worries at the moment, though. There was too much to do. With my entrance interviews out of the way and the results of my physical exam finally in, my acceptance to The Citadel was now official. I had less than two months to get ready for the greatest battle I had yet faced. I could not afford to fail. It might be my only chance.

★ CHAPTER 2 ★

1800 BULLDOGS AND 4 BITCHES

In some respects, leaving for my first day of college was no different from any other new freshman's. I finished packing my bags, kissed my dog Karo good-bye, and watched as my father loaded my belongings into the trunk of our light blue Cadillac with the personalized Citadel plates. One difference, however, would have been obvious to any onlooker. Most freshmen don't have a camera crew in the backseat of the family car and a second camera unit trailing them in a van. At The Citadel's request, I had reluctantly agreed to let "48 Hours" do a segment on my departure for college, which accounted for the microphones recording my every word as we pulled away from the house. My mind wasn't on the cameras, though. I could think of nothing but what awaited me behind the black iron gates of my new college.

I leaned over my mother's shoulder for most of the drive, straining to catch my first glimpse of the familiar white-turreted walls as I answered the reporter's occasional questions. I had pulled my long brown hair back into a ponytail, knowing it might be the last time in four years that my hair would be long enough to secure with a hair band. I was so worked up, it was hard to sit still, and I tapped my athletic shoes nervously on the floor of the car as my father drove. We had gotten away shortly after sunrise for the twenty-five mile drive to the College. As I scanned the horizon that morning, I asked my mother if she was going to cry when it came time to say good-bye. I didn't want her to embarrass me in front of the cadets; more important, I didn't want to embarrass myself by bursting into tears along with her.

As we drove down the interstate and into the heart of old Charleston, I could barely contain my nervous excitement. The familiar streets began to narrow as we wound through the once-proud neighborhoods bordering Hampton Park. Run-down brick and wooden two-story buildings, all with the wide covered porches so typical of Charleston, were mixed with newly restored turn-of-the-century homes and peeling storefront churches. I had made this drive dozens of times that summer, but this journey was different. This time I would not be visiting my father's *alma mater*. This time I would be entering my own college.

As we neared the campus, I saw the familiar Citadel flag flying from a pole on the front porch of a neighboring house. Noticing something odd about the banner, I squinted into the sun. Attached to the flagpole were several pink ribbons, fluttering gently in the early morning breeze. My spirits soared, and I grinned. I knew those ribbons were for me.

It wasn't until we passed the edge of the park that I saw the crowds.

They were everywhere, clustered around the black iron gates of the College like a flock of chickens at feeding time. About a dozen members of a local feminist group, including women, men, and a few children, held up banners with slogans like YOU GO, GIRL CADETS! The vast majority of the crowd, however, was from the media: Cars, vans, reporters with microphones, and camera operators with cords trailing in every direction descended on our car, all competing for a glimpse of me and the other three female freshmen scheduled to arrive that day. I ignored the reporters as my father gave my name and barracks assignment to the cadet guard on duty at the gate, and we drove on through.

Once inside, it seemed as though everything speeded up. The press had already been told that they would not be allowed to interview any of the females, or any other freshman for that matter, so I was able to go about the business of checking in without being bothered by reporters. I was to live in 2nd Battalion, the Padgett–Thomas Barracks, along with the other three women who were entering with me. A girl named Kim Messer and I would room together. I had already met Kim, and though I had my doubts about her attitude toward cadet life, because she had agreed to do some media events prior to entering school, I was hoping for the best. The other two women freshmen would share a room a few doors down from us: a girl named Petra Lovetinska, the daughter of a Czeck Embassy employee, who was attending the college on an alumni scholarship, and another female, Jeanie Mentlavos, the younger sister of a senior Citadel cadet. A women's restroom had been built for us off the gallery near our rooms, with shower stalls and a lock on the door. The local newscast had shown carpenters drilling holes for the LADIES' ROOM sign only the night before.

A cadet corporal named Mr. Sharp helped Dad and me unload my bags and showed us to my room. My mother would not be coming with us. Citadel tradition said that only fathers could accompany arriving freshmen into the barracks. I didn't question that tradition as I was shown to my quarters. I had come to El Cid to follow in my father's footsteps, and I was overwhelmed with pride as my father helped me carry my bags through the side sally port on that hot August morning. I already knew what was waiting for me there.

Like every other cadet in the Corps, I was assigned to the barest military quarters imaginable. The only difference between my room and the hundreds of others in Padgett–Thomas Barracks was the blinds on the window and the sliding bolt on the inside of my door. In every other way, my new room couldn't have been further from the white brass daybed piled with pillows and surrounded by family mementos that I had left at home in Goose Creek.

The room itself was small, less than eighteen feet by ten feet, its drab walls bluish white in the sun filtering through the window over the door. To my left was a small sink with a storage cabinet below. Next to the sink were the two open metal structures, called "full-presses" in Citadel lingo, which would serve as our closets. Both were painted army tan, six feet high, and scarred with the nicks and dents of several generations of cadets. Almost touching the full-presses was a half-press, a sort of metal chest of drawers, that would serve as Kim's dresser. It stood about half the height of the full-press. In the left-hand corner, just under the window, was a plain metal study desk with a small lamp. Directly across from it, on the opposite wall, was an identical metal desk shoved into the other corner. Above and in between the two desks was the window, already damp with humidity. There was just enough room for Kim and me to pull out our desk chairs without bumping into each other from behind.

Next to the right-hand desk was another half-press, exactly like its twin on the opposite wall, that would be my dresser. This half-press stood next to the bunk bed—called racks—that Kim and I would be sharing. Like everything else in the room, the bed frame was a battered metal structure with just enough room for two thin, narrow, thirty-inch mattresses. Apparently the College thought that if the beds were too comfortable, cadets would be less willing to get up before dawn. Completing the layout was a rifle rack at the head of the bed and a metal trash can. Well, at least I wouldn't have to worry about breaking anything.

One part of the moving-in ritual that morning was the "Room Responsibility" form Mr. Sharp asked me to sign. The last item was hilarious. The form required me not only to verify that the furniture and lights were in "OK" condition, but that the room had four walls! I had to sign a promise to return the walls at the end of the semester. What did the College think I was going to do, drop out and take one of the walls with me?

Barely glancing around, Dad dropped my large duffel bag on the floor and said that he and my mother would meet me outside for lunch in the Mess Hall. Afterward, as we both knew, I would be marched away with the other freshmen, where I wouldn't be allowed to see or talk to my parents until Hell Week was over. Removing the cigar from his mouth for a moment, my father nodded matter-of-factly at me and walked out. Mr. Sharp handed me a list of "Academic Orientation

Rules" and told me to pick up my supply box in the quad and change into my PTs (Physical Training uniform) before leaving the barracks. Then he said, "You're on your own now," and followed my father out the door.

For a few moments, I just stood there, staring in silence at my surroundings. A less homelike living space could hardly be imagined. Everything was metal, everything was scarred, everything was a putrid faded tan, with the exception of the walls, which already bore the signs of Charleston mildew in spite of being recently painted a pale Citadel blue. None of this bothered me, however. I liked the idea of roughing it as my father had—for all I knew, with the very same furniture. Beat-up furniture was the least of my worries.

I looked down at the list of rules in my hand. There were seven of them. During Academic Orientation I was not to use the vending machines or pay phones, talk or socialize on the galleries of the barracks, or speak to any upperclassman who was not on the academic staff. I was to wear full PTs at all times, and once my family left, I was not allowed to leave my room unless told to do so. There was one exception: I was allowed to use the bathroom whenever necessary. "No problem," I thought, "I can do that." So far, so good.

A few minutes later, I reported to the table in the quad to sign in and pick up my supply box. Until Monday, when our duty uniforms would be issued, I would have to wear my summer PTs everywhere on campus. I signed my name and was told to take one of the large cardboard boxes on the nearby table back to my quarters. I glanced inside as I picked it up. The box contained the basics of cadet life: bedspreads, blankets, hangers, desk pads, shoulder boards, breast plates, and so on and so on. Clutching the box to my chest, I thought that there were some advantages to being flat-chested. A bigger chest would have made lugging the heavy box around even more difficult than it was. Struggling to balance it, I was relieved to cover the distance back to my quarters without dropping anything.

Once there, I carefully arranged the items in my desk and presses, then did my best to make up my rack. Contoured sheets are forbidden at The Citadel, and in spite of my best efforts, the military corners I tried to construct with the flat sheets looked uneven. Sighing philosophically, I told myself that I'd soon get the hang of it. My duffel was next, and as I unpacked the large duffel my dad had left for me, I couldn't help smiling when I reached the bottom. There were the items that had not been on The Citadel freshman list: my bras and tampons. As I unpacked the sports bras and placed them in the drawer, I reflected that there were some differences from my male classmates that were never going to change.

As I pulled off my civilian clothes to put on my first cadet uniform, I thought back to the day I was six years old and put on my first Citadel T-shirt. I had come a long way already, for this was no souvenir I was pulling over my head: It was the real deal. As I slipped on the dark blue shorts and T-shirt with the College logo, my hands shook with excitement. Pulling my hair back into a ponytail, I debated whether or not to put on leggings under my shorts. The new rules for women said we had to wear spandex for modesty under our PT shorts, but it was already hot outside, and the shorts bagged halfway to my knees. Knotting my athletic shoes, I returned to the quad and approached the cadet who had checked me in at the table, to ask if I needed to put on leggings. He looked at me like I was crazy and shouted, "Tuck your shirt in!" I was embarrassed and shocked by his rudeness, but of course, I quickly did as he asked. I decided against the leggings.

As I made my way across the quad, I saw another young woman approaching me. I recognized her from newspaper photos as Jeanie Mentlavos, another of the female freshmen. Grinning broadly at the sight of a sister knob (as they called Citadel freshmen), I stuck my hand out and greeted her warmly. Jeanie, her pretty brunette features flushed with excitement, shook my hand with equal warmth. As our hands met, I saw the flash of cameras go off through the entrance to the barracks. Ignoring them, I told Jeanie I'd see her in a little while.

A small group of us, family and new friends, walked into the Mess Hall together. There is nothing inviting about the campus Mess Hall. The hall is huge and severely plain. Like most everything else at The Citadel, the walls are a dull grayish white, which makes the room seem even bigger. Lining the walls on one side are flags representing the nation, the state, and the College. Like every other room at The Citadel, the Mess Hall contains many large portraits of former cadets and administrators. The tables themselves, which seat fourteen, are made of heavy dark wood, cut in a plain block style, with three-by-three-inch legs and absolutely no decorative touches. The chairs are equally plain, made of heavy dark wood with rigidly straight backs. Not the kind of chair to eat comfortably in, but then that's the idea. Mealtimes in the Corps have nothing to do with comfort.

The next stop was the Band Hall, for a continental breakfast with my family. A couple of dozen new cadets were auditioning. After considerable thought, I had auditioned for a spot playing the clarinet that summer. I thought that playing a musical instrument would be a good psychological and artistic outlet for the stress of cadet life. Major Day, the band director, had said I wasn't ready for Carnegie Hall, but that I was "good enough" and would get better. Looking at the nervous freshmen waiting to audition nearby, I was glad I had successfully completed my own audition that summer.

In typical fashion, my mother was already making friends. My dad sat watching the scene quietly, his eyes lighting with amusement now and then, the eternal cigar sticking out of the corner of his mouth— unlit, of course. I met several parents and their freshman sons, and we all started talking. Most of the other freshmen were too nervous themselves to worry about whether or not I was a female. Among the group was Alex Sparra, who would soon become my good friend, and his mother, Pat Scanlan, who formed a kind of support team with my mother. The other cadets were only faces at the time, but they would soon become almost as familiar to me as the faces of my brother and sisters.

After the auditions, we all walked to the Mess Hall for the traditional freshman-parent lunch. On the way, I stopped for a moment to stick my head in the door of my room. Still empty. By now it was nearly 11 A.M., and Kim still had not arrived. Not a good start to the semester.

Saturday lunch mess is the moment when freshmen separate from their families and begin academic orientation. My family and I grouped ourselves around the tables and walls, listening attentively as Colonel Trez welcomed us all to the College, made a few announcements, and then turned the microphone over to the chaplain for the blessing of the food. A few moments later, the parents were invited to a nicely spread buffet table to fill their plates; once the parents were served, the cadets were told to serve themselves, upperclassmen first. It was our first lesson in good manners. The freshmen and their families introduced themselves to one another and chatted excitedly. I was so excited, and so nervous, that I could barely sit still, much less eat. If I'd known I would spend the next few months hungry, I would have tried harder.

After we finished eating, Colonel Trez told us to say good-bye and proceed to Mark Clark Hall for the first session. That meant saying good-bye to my parents, for the first time in my life. None of us would be allowed to speak to our parents until the first week was behind us, nor allowed to see them until well after that. I could see my mother swallowing tears as she hugged me. I bit my lip and tried not to cry as I felt her arms around me. My dad, on the other hand, simply stuck out his hand and growled in his trademark rumble, "I don't want to see or hear from you until Parents' Day. If you decide to quit, don't call me to come get you. Just put on your jogging shoes and start walking home." I asked him what was going to happen to me on Hell Night a few days later. He just laughed and told me I would find out soon enough. And with that, he and my mother left. On the way out, my parents made their only formal statement to the press that day. It was, my father said, "going very well, just as planned." The rest was up to me.

I actually enjoyed the rest of the day. There were cameras everywhere, with flashbulbs going off in my face every time I turned around, but I didn't care. Let them take all the pictures they wanted. In between meetings, I ran into Petra Lovetinska, and we introduced ourselves. A tall, red-haired Czechoslovakian tomboy, she greeted me with a friendly handshake. I liked her immediately. I also learned that my roommate Kim had arrived just before lunch, having been given the wrong check-in time. As I moved from one orientation meeting to another, I found myself grinning with excitement. Late in the afternoon, not long before dinner, we all went into the chapel for a short inspirational meeting. I sat with the other freshmen in the silence of the fading afternoon, staring up at the rainbow of colored glass above the altar. "How beautiful," I thought, and my heart filled with peace. The evening was spent in the auditorium with other freshmen watching an improv group called the Have Not's. We had a great time.

Only two things made me stop smiling that day. One was my company operations sergeant, Mr. Wizeman, who reprimanded me twice for minor infractions. He kept staring at me with solemn brown eyes, and I felt intimidated. I wondered what he was thinking. It made me uncomfortable. The other shadow on the day was one that would soon loom large in my life—my roommate, Kim.

For starters, she smoked. I asked her very politely not to do so in our room, and she promised she wouldn't, but when I returned to our room after an errand, I could smell smoke in the air. Clearly, Kim had no intention of honoring her promise. My mother had lost part of one lung to illness just a few years before, and I worried about breathing cigarette smoke day after day. Worse, it was only our first night in the barracks, and she got me in trouble. While I was gone to the restroom, Kim left our room for half an hour, leaving the door standing open. I returned to find an angry cadet officer in our doorway, who gave me heat for the open door. Even though I wasn't responsible for the infraction, I had no choice but to respond, "Sir, no excuse, sir." Kim just shrugged when I told her later what had happened, and it really pissed me off. She could at least have apologized for getting me in trouble. I tried to tell myself that we had just gotten off to a bad start, that things would improve, but I already had a growing knot in my stomach whenever I looked at my roommate. There was an arrogance about her that seemed to hang in the air.

I spent the rest of the first evening writing out the names of the Regimental staff, Band cadet rank-holders, and the Table of Organization and Equipment (TO&E), knowing I'd have to recite both from memory in the next few days. I was already worried about keeping up with all of the required memorization, even more worried that I wouldn't be able to concentrate with the constant noise and confusion of knob life. It would take everything I'd learned about coping with ADD if I was going to survive.

In spite of these problems, however, my first day at The Citadel had gone surprisingly well. As I lay in bed that first night, gazing out the open window at the mist rising from the Parade Field, the sound of taps came drifting in, a sweet benediction to the excitement of the day. Filled with hope, I fell into a deep, peaceful sleep, the narrow mattress underneath me supporting my tired body like a strong hand.

Sunday dawned bright and beautiful. At 0900 (9 A.M. civilian time) Kim and I, along with several hundred of our fellow knobs, sat in Summerall Chapel waiting for protestant services to begin. Out of the corner of my eye, I saw my parents enter the chapel and take a seat across the aisle. They both knew that I would not be allowed to speak to them, but they had come anyway, in a show of psychological support. I lowered my head for a moment and smiled as I registered their presence.

That first Sunday, chapel was very informal, sort of a "Come to Jesus" service of encouragement given by the chaplain and cadre. The sanctuary was crowded with the families of freshman students, some parents even standing in the back when seating ran out. As I bowed my head, the chaplain offered up a prayer for us freshmen, that we could survive the hardships of the coming weeks. I had been praying that same prayer all summer, on my knees at home with a family rosary clutched in my fingers. Afterward, Cadet Captain Shaun King spoke. After jokingly opening with the words, "Believe me, knobs, you're going to need all the prayers you can get," he continued in a more serious tone. "When you finish your knob year, you know that you really got through something that no one can take away from you. But it's a matter of personal motivation." The message was clear: The challenge before us was difficult, but not impossible. And only in overcoming those obstacles could we find the inner strength not only to be Citadel cadets, but to be strong, successful human beings. While I listened to his words, I felt a thrill of hope and determination surge through my body. I would be here again the following summer, and the one after that, until I won whatever battles I might face.

Emerging from the chapel an hour later, surrounded by the other freshmen, I could see the lines of anxious parents ringed around the sidewalk and parking spaces below, each straining for a glimpse of their son or daughter's face. I could not find my parents' faces in the crowd, but as cadet officers herded us down the chapel steps and back to the barracks, I heard a familiar voice ring out behind me. It was my mother's: "Go, Mace, go!" she shouted, and a moment later, I heard my father rumble, "Run, Mace!" Unable to conceal a grin, I fell into formation and jogged toward my new home. Somebody loved me. I wasn't going to let them down.

That Sunday night was my last evening as a "civilian." The next day

I would enter the dark tunnel known as Hell Week; within twenty-four hours, I would be one of the first four women ever to take The Citadel Cadet Oath. I tried to shut these events out of my mind as I lay in bed, once again willing the sound of the bugle to sing me to sleep. This time, however, sleep wasn't so quick in coming.

★ CHAPTER 3 ★

NANCY THE KNOB

None of us slept well on that first Sunday night. Yet, in spite of my nerves, I found myself drifting off a couple of hours before dawn. Unfortunately, just as I got comfortable, I was ejected from my thin, narrow mattress into a world unlike anything I had ever imagined.

I never really understood the meaning of "rude awakening" until I began Hell Week at The Citadel. Technically, the correct term for those first five days of military training is "Cadre Week," referring to the group of cadets who train freshmen, but no knob who survives it remembers that week as anything but sheer hell. The first day is a series of humiliations that leaves you confused, frustrated, exhausted, and worst of all, nearly bald. And it all begins before 0530, 5:30 A.M. civilian time, with a wake-up call from hell. So much for my little iron daybed and my mother's voice calling me to breakfast at home. This Monday morning I was roused from sleep before dawn by AC/DC's version of "Hell's Bells," bursting out of the loudspeakers at earsplitting decibels, and someone pounding on my door, shouting, "Get up, knobs!" I would never have believed it, but that turned out to be the best part of my day.

The cadre were already pumped and ready for action by the time I threw my clothes on and raced for the door. They had already circled the Parade ground twice, shouting and clapping, so their vocal cords were loose and ready to raise the dead. By 0600 they were herding us down the street at a sharp clip in front of Barracks 2 and around another corner to the Mess Hall. The warm, damp air clung to my body, and moisture ran down the rows of windows as we trooped by. Everything was gray and shadowy, with mist shrouding the ghostly white walls around us. I had leapt from bed grinning with excitement. For the first time, a tiny knot of anxiety began to form itself in my stomach.

Arriving at the Mess Hall didn't make me feel any better. The long white hall echoed with the shouts of cadre, and the odor of nervous perspiration was already filling the air. Standing at attention next to a heavy, stiff-backed wooden chair, I kept my eyes straight ahead and waited for the order to sit. The moment I did, the table was surrounded by dark-faced women in navy blue dresses and aprons, their hair covered with nets, who swiftly and efficiently set platters and pitchers in front of us, family-style. These were The Citadel "waitees." The waitees were the only other women I could see in the entire hall. Testosterone hung in the air as thick as the South Carolina mist.

Perched awkwardly on the edge of my chair, I peered from the corners of my eyes at the food the women had piled on the table: pale pancakes, bowls of sugary cereal, limp bacon, runny grits, pitchers filled with liquid in a strange orange shade I had never seen before. When I took my first uncertain sip, it was clear why drinks in the Mess Hall were referred to by color only, as they didn't taste like any flavor I had ever swallowed. And even if the bland and greasy food had been even slightly appetizing, the constant noise and the knot in my stomach under the glare of our mess carver destroyed any trace of appetite. Hungry or not, I soon learned, I would be forced to swallow every morsel of the sludge they placed in front of me, three meals a day. Chewing was something else again; we were ordered to chew each mouthful exactly three times, regardless of what the food was. But swallow we must, whether it came to the food or the sarcastic remarks of the cadet who criticized our every move, forcing us to choke down mouthfuls in time to say, "Sir, yes, sir," in response to his orders and remarks. Glancing down the table, I wondered if my own face looked as worried as the pale, sweaty faces of the other knobs.

The air was already steamy with the South Carolina heat as we trooped off once again, this time to Mark Clark Hall for yet another freshman assembly. While the cadre waited outside, their black caps pulled down to the frown lines above their eyebrows, the knobs gathered in the auditorium for a final pep talk before facing the terror that awaited us outside. After an official welcome by Colonel Trez and a long series of announcements and last minute reminders, the tall, dignified figure of Cadet Colonel Bryant Butler stepped up to the microphone for a final speech before we were dismissed. His words were brief but to the point, ending with this encouragement: "I know you're scared," he told us, his black face solemn and his eyes intense. "Remember, it's not impossible. You can make it." And with those words, we were ordered to report immediately to the cadet officers waiting for us outside. I took a deep breath and filed behind the others out into the sunshine.

On the steps outside the hall, several dozen cadet officers awaited us, brown clipboards in their white-gloved hands. On the backs of the clipboards were letters made of white tape, each forming one of the seventeen company symbols. As I came down the steps toward the street, surrounded by more than five hundred other freshmen, I could see the cadet officer with the Band Company clipboard a couple of dozen yards away, near the edge of the Parade Field. The first three freshman to arrive were already lined up next to each other; as the rest of us reported, we were ordered to stand directly behind one of the three. Once all twenty-five Band Company knobs had taken their places in the three lines, the officer in charge began reading out our names. When he came to Mace, I sang out, "Sir, yes, sir," in a voice I hoped sounded strong and confident. Around me hundreds of deeper male voices responded with the same words. Within a short time, the crowd of milling bodies had settled into stiff, silent formations, bodies tense and eyes fixed straight ahead. Out of the corners of my eyes, I could see camera lights flashing in the distance. I knew that many of those cameras were directed at me. I paid no attention. Military training had officially begun.

No need to wonder what was coming next. Everyone on campus knew. The barber shop. Since we'd first trooped off to the Mess Hall, reporters had lined the street in front of Mark Clark Hall, under the watchful eyes of Citadel officials, hoping to get a last picture of us females before our hair was chopped off. The reporters would not be allowed to get near the barber shop, but they were still hoping to get a good before-and-after picture for the next day's feature story. Nothing since my arrival had excited as much interest as the women's haircuts. As I stood in line outside Mark Clark Hall, waiting for my turn in the barber's chair, I could see the curious faces of food workers staring at me through the windows of the nearby canteen, where guests and staff members were still eating breakfast. Rumors were running wild: Would our hair really be shaved off? And if not, just how much of our hair would be cut? I'd seen the pictures of the new cut, but pictures were one thing. Having my hair buzzed off was another.

While I waited, I considered the challenge before me. This was the moment I had been rehearsing for—for nearly two months. Citadel officials had asked me to be the guinea pig—a model, to be politically correct—for the new female haircut. Several possibilities had been tried out, using a computer-imaged haircut from my head. When the decision was finally made, I tried to imagine how it would feel when my long hair fell to the ground, and reassured myself countless times that I was ready to be transformed into a "knob," the word used to describe the hairless state of Citadel freshmen. Both Kim and Jeanie had cut their hair earlier that summer, to get used to having shorter hair. I, however, had deliberately left my hair long. I knew how traumatic the haircut was for many male freshmen, and I wanted to experience the same sense of shock they did when watching their hair fall to the floor. It seemed only fair. One thing I was certain of: I was not going to cry. I felt strong, pumped up for the ordeal that awaited me. The administration had made sure the media could not record the actual cutting, but it wasn't the media I cared about. If I was going to be accepted by the other cadets, crying like a girl while my head was buzzed was out of the question.

Usually the companies received their haircuts in alphabetical order, with Band Company second in line, but this year we were first, making me the first female cadet in the barber's chair. As I was ordered through the door amid the hum of clippers, I was surrounded by a small army of anxious College officials, all there to watch the historic moment. I stared stoically ahead, unmoving, as the barber, Dave Creaturo, sliced through the hair at the base of my neck. Everyone, especially the barber, treated me with sympathetic concern, but they needn't have worried. I felt quite relaxed as Mr. Creaturo snipped away. In fact, I thought it was funny that the officers watching my haircut looked more nervous than I did. I was the guinea pig, and when Mr. Creaturo had cut my hair down to less than two inches all over, the officials moved closer to look at the result. After a brief conference, they all agreed: Not short enough. Mr. Creaturo cut it again. A second inspection produced the same result: Still not short enough. Time dragged on, and in the mirror I could see the other knobs climbing in and out of the chairs next to me for three-minute buzzes while the barber continued to clip away at my head. By the time he reached the twenty-minute mark, I just wanted him to finish. For one thing, I was dying to go to the bathroom, and it was beginning to feel like I would be stuck in that chair all morning. Finally, he stepped back, and this time the administrators surveyed me with satisfaction.

The reflection I saw in the mirror showed me that the old Nancy was gone; in her place was Nancy the Knob, the spitting image of my brother James. The hair on my crown had been trimmed to a half inch in length, the sides were tapered like a boy's to almost bare skin above my ears, and the hair at the back of my neck had been tapered short. In the paper the next day, a cadet officer who had watched the process was quoted as saying, "I didn't think it would be that short. It is not very flattering at all." No kidding. I swallowed hard and got out of the chair. Well, I had wanted a new start. There was no turning back now. I emerged from the shop transformed into a knob, a freshman without gender. I later learned that one of my own classmates didn't recognize me. He thought I was just another male knob, waiting to have my head shaved. It would be a long time before I looked like a girl again.

A few minutes later, Petra, in what I soon learned was typical fashion, strode in, sat down in the barber chair, and said, "Cut it all off!" Neither Kim nor Jeanie was able to handle it as calmly. Both of them broke down in tears as their hair was sheared off, with the sympathetic barber handing them paper towels to wipe their faces as they got out of the chair. Kim's parents watched from the street as Kim emerged through the glass doors with damp eyes, loyally telling reporters that they thought Kim looked just fine. Just at that moment, a freelance news photographer slipped through the ropes restricting the press and snapped a picture of Kim's tearful face. Furious, Citadel administrators showed him to the gate and ordered the TV crews off the Parade Field, where they waited to film our military training. I didn't blame Kim for crying. There was no real disgrace in shedding a few tears in the barber shop, I knew, for some of the male cadets had cried even harder than Kim or Jeanie did when their hair was shaved. Still, I was proud of myself for staying strong under the pressure of the moment. I had set a higher standard for myself than for the male knobs, for I knew that the standard applied to males would never be applied to me. I would have to be twice as good, twice as tough, if I hoped for any respect in the Corps.

Meanwhile, I found a way to cope with my new look. I just didn't look in the mirror. Ever. It was more than a week before I looked in a mirror again, and then only to perform necessary hygiene. The last thing a knob needed to worry about was looking pretty, I told myself. That would have to wait for another day.

It would be a long, long wait.

★ CHAPTER 4 ★

THE HAZE MAZE

The buildup to the haircut had been so intense that when it was over, and I had survived without weakening, I thought the worst of the day was over. I could not have been more wrong. The day had barely begun.

After being walked in formation back to our barracks, the company officers ordered us to line up between the pillars on the quad, next to the Band Company letters, for the official signing in to our company. We were told to remain in line until our names were called. Meanwhile, the cadre gave us our first lesson in proper military behavior.

The first movement every cadet is taught is the salute, the most basic gesture of respect for a soldier. After carefully explaining and demonstrating the proper way to salute, we were each ordered to salute the cadre. To my embarrassment, I could not make my hand and arm duplicate the gesture I had just seen demonstrated. Eighteen years living on a military base, yet I, the general's daughter, had delivered a snappier salute at five years old. Clearly disgusted by my pathetic performance, the cadet training officer adjusted my elbow and fingers, trying to mold my hand into the correct position. Again and again I saluted him, and again and again he had to reposition my hand. If I accidentally moved before he instructed me, he would lean in close and scream, "Don't move! Don't frickin' move! Did I tell you to move?" And if I inadvertently glanced at him for clarification, I was greeted with, "Quit looking at me, smack! You don't look at me! Who do you think you are?" I was mortified. All the while there were other cadre around us, two or three to a knob, moving around and down the line so each knob was getting yelled at from all sides. They seemed to be coming from all angles, instructing and yelling. I made a mental note right then to practice my salute in front of the mirror that night.

As I struggled to follow the cadet's instructions, I was aware of the cameras peering through the back sally port, taping the entire process. One of the cameras was fixed on me, another on my roommate. I recognized the "48 Hours" cameraman a few yards away. I desperately hoped no one else realized that he was there for me. Meanwhile, one by one, each knob was called to the company table for the signing-in ritual.

Signing in to your company is the first of many "games" designed to test freshmen psychologically. Unfortunately, no one tells you that ahead of time. The process seemed simple enough: As each of our names was called, we had to approach the table where our first sergeant sat, put our feet on the taped line, salute the cadet, and sign the document that made us members of Band Company. The only catch, as far as I could see, was that there seemed to be an unusually long reach from the taped line to the table. Apart from that, it didn't seem hard. Yeah, right.

When Mr. Rawlinson, the company first sergeant, called, "Mace!" I stepped forward to sign my name on the roster, my heart beating with excitement. The minute I got near the table, I was loudly ordered to keep my feet behind the line while I signed my name. This meant that my arms would barely reach the table. "As long as I don't lose my balance," I thought, "I should be fine." I snapped to attention and gave the cadet 1st sergeant my best salute. Sadly, my best salute was pitiful. I was ordered to about-face, step away from the table, return, and give a proper salute this time. Once again, I tried and failed. Nearby, cadre screamed at other knobs. I struggled to concentrate in the chaos. After several tries and a lot of shouting from the cadet behind the table, I was finally allowed to continue.

The moment I bent to pick up the pen, however, I encountered the second obstacle in the stress test. The officer barked out, "Don't touch that table, knob! This is the 1st sergeant's table." I was ordered to leave yet again and return immediately, and this time to "Get it right!" This time around I planted my toes behind the line and leaned cautiously forward, carefully grasping one of the pens that lay next to the roster. Catch number three: I couldn't lift the pen (I later learned that it had been glued to the table). While I stared in astonishment, the cadet officers around the table began yelling at me at the top of their lungs, ridiculing me because I was too big a wimp to lift a pen. All of them began shouting different orders at the same time, and I didn't know which one to listen to. Shaken by their anger, and frustrated by my failure to do something so simple, I left the table and returned again. This time I picked up a different pen without either crossing the line or touching the table, but even then, there was a catch: The pen was out of ink. More screaming in my face. On the next try I found a pen that worked, but just as I finished the loop on the "y" of my first name, I was told that time was up. Once again, I had failed. I was sent away, then told to return, running the entire time, while the cadets continued to shout and criticize my every move.

By then I was sweating heavily, and my hand was beginning to shake. I was having my first encounter with Cadre 101: Confuse and confound. By then I was so exhausted and confused that I could hardly sign my own name. After what seemed like forever, I finally managed to scrawl my signature within the allowed time and was sent back to my platoon. Heaving a sigh of relief, I waited for my breathing to slow and repeated the advice my father had given me, over and over in my head: "It's only a game. They're just playing with you." And they were. Looking back, the whole ridiculous routine, complete with glued pens, seems funny. At the time, though, it didn't seem funny at all.

One by one, every freshman in Band Company signed his name. It took over an hour. It was now almost 0900.

If signing in to our companies was our first lesson in harassment, collecting our uniforms was the second. No sooner had we officially signed into our companies than we were marched over to the Cadet Store to begin what the Corps calls the "Haze Maze."

The "Haze Maze" begins innocently enough, at the door of the Cadet Store, by the green fields at the back of the campus that lie parallel to the Ashley River. The store lies near one of The Citadel's minor tourist attractions, a small hump of ground that is the highest point of land in Charleston. Visitors from out of state think it's hilarious that this lump of grass is the closest thing Charleston has to a mountain. Our newly shaved heads covered by baseball caps, my company reassembled inside the barracks and was marched the quarter mile to the cadet store. We trooped past the "hill" to our cadre's cadence and lined up for our uniform issue outside the door, less than a hundred yards from the marshes where my father had once poached alligators. We would start collecting our uniform pieces in the Cadet Store and end in the Tailor Shop, where we would be measured for our hats, jackets, shirts, and pants.

It sounded simple enough: moving from station to station, one knob at a time, to either be issued an article of clothing or be measured for one. As I stood at attention with the rest of my company, the *Guidon* held rigidly in my left hand, I wasn't worried about the process I was about to begin. I was more concerned about the aching in my arm from long minutes of holding the handbook at eye level while sweat trickled down my neck. The temperature was already nudging toward 90, and it wasn't even noon yet.

When it was my turn, I stepped from the muggy heat of the riverside into the entranceway. A male voice abruptly ordered me to halt. Demanding that I sound off my name, he located my nametag on the table next to him, handed it to me, and ordered me to pin it on my shirt. Then, pointing to a cadet a few yards farther ahead, he told me to proceed to the next station. Saluting him awkwardly, I moved stiffly toward the cadet he had pointed out. I didn't know it yet, but I was entering the first step in the Haze Maze.

The moment I came within a few feet of the next cadet his voice rang out, yelling at me for stepping on the line. What line? Glancing down, I could see that my feet were planted on the perimeter of a small square of masking tape, mounted on the floor beneath me. I abruptly stepped back inside the square, to be criticized once again for moving without orders. By then the cadet could read my nametag, so this time his sarcasm was personal. My eyes straight ahead, I could see a series of the small squares, taped to the floor all around me in an apparently random order. I had no time to consider the pattern. I was immediately ordered forward to be issued another item.

The next thing I was given was a white canvas bag, into which all my other uniform articles would be deposited. The bag would serve as the laundry bag for my clothing. Item by item, the bag would be filled that morning until it weighed over forty pounds. As I blinked in the shadows, trying to get my contact lenses to adjust to the light, I could see other knobs moving stiffly from station to station, standing at attention as they waited for instructions or the next item for their laundry bag. To my surprise, the noise level around me rivaled the commotion of a department store on the day after Thanksgiving. I moved forward on order to receive my first article of clothing, a terry cloth robe to wear to the showers, when I felt an explosion of hot breath on my cheek and a voice screamed in my ear. My body involuntarily flinched.

It is difficult to explain how a simple shopping expedition could become one of the most stressful hours of my life. Yet, inside the store, cadre members paced from knob to knob, shouting confusing instructions at the top of their lungs, yelling at us to stand up straighter, screaming questions faster than we could answer them. After a while, it all became a blur as I was ordered from station to station, shouting out, "Sir, yes, sir," "Sir, no, sir," "Sir, no excuse, sir," as I tried to keep my wits together and collect each item.

I already knew there would be problems fitting me. Two weeks earlier, I had learned that the black leather military shoes I had so carefully broken in that summer were unacceptable. Apparently, the style of the toes did not fit Citadel requirements. I had been measured for a new pair of shoes, which had to be specially ordered, as nothing in stock was small enough for me. I had already picked up the shoes, which felt stiff and awkward on my swelling feet. Blisters were certain; I only hoped I could keep them from becoming infected. As it turned out, the shoe problem was only the beginning. Nothing in the Cadet Store fitted me properly; even the extra-small items were too big, and cut to fit a male. The belt they issued me could be wrapped another quarter of the way around my skinny waist, and my new hat sank low over my ears. I could already imagine the racking I would receive for my "sloppy" uniform.

By the time I had inched my way from square to square across the Cadet Store, my nerves were raw. Emerging once again into the sunlight, I waited outside with the rest of my company, sipping water and reading my *Guidon* at attention, as the other knobs inched painfully through the maze inside. One poor knob, his face filled with misery, held his left hand over his bald head as he read his *Guidon*. He had forgotten to put on his cover (hat). Sweat poured down his face and neck as he squinted at the words on the page in front of him. When everyone had made his way through, we were marched to the Tailor Shop next door, to be measured for our dress uniforms. Once inside, I was ordered to take a seat in a row of chairs occupied by other knobs. Like them, I perched carefully on the edge of the seat, back straight, forearm at a ninety-degree angle to the floor, clutched my *Guidon* in my hand, and began reading. In the comparative quiet of the Tailor Shop, I was shocked to hear the sound of a young male sobbing. I had rarely ever heard a boy my age cry. Male voices, raised in anger, screamed at an unseen freshman. One voice demanded to know the rank depicted on each jacket. "Hey, smack, what rank is this cadet uniform? Answer me, knob! Don't you know, knob? What's wrong, are you stupid, knob?"

For the first time since arriving at The Citadel, I fought to keep back tears. Exhausted from an hour of nonstop harassment, I was caught off guard by the sound of a boy sobbing behind me. All of a sudden, I felt sick. I just wanted to get out of that room, out of the endless maze of noise and confusion. I felt as though my head was spinning. Before I left, though, I had to be fitted for my duty uniform. I bit my lip and stepped forward when I heard my name. While I stood there being measured, Mr. Hood's hot breath exploding in my face, I thought about how excited I'd been to get the traditional gray trousers and shirt. At that moment, however, I felt anything but excited. Stuttering in confusion as I tried to identify the insignias Mr. Hood pointed out, it was all I could do to keep my own tears back. It was like elementary school all over again. Under Mr. Hood's constant pressure, I couldn't even think straight.

When I finally emerged from my fitting into the bright noonday sun, holding the forty-pound canvas bag straight out in front of me, I wondered for the first time what I had really gotten myself into. Twenty-four hours later, I would learn that the cadet crying in the Tailor Shop was the first freshman to quit that semester.

If I had to choose the hardest part of that first day of Hell Week, it wouldn't be either the physical strain or the constant racking. The hardest part was that the pressure never stopped, never for a single minute. There was never a moment to gather my wits, catch my breath, think my own thoughts. Every second of my existence was controlled by someone else. By the time I had carried the heavy canvas bag back to my quarters in the barracks, it was time to form up for the march to lunch.

I'd like to say that lunch was a chance for us all to rest. Not even close. The worst meal of my life was that lunch mess with Cadet 1st Sergeant Rawlinson. Mr. Rawlinson was a very tall, very muscular, very intimidating officer with a dark stoical face and veiled eyes that gave no hint of what he was thinking. He was not only intimidating; he was also extremely intelligent, and he used his intelligence to play with our minds. For no apparent reason, except that I was the only female in Band Company, Mr. Rawlinson already had me pegged as a "gaudy knob," a girl with an attitude, and he had no patience with attitude.

The moment I sat down for the noon meal that first day he began racking the piss out of me. He seethed questions at me one after the other, and he didn't like my answers to any of them. "Why did you really come here, Mace? Why don't you just leave, Mace? Do you think you're something special, smack? What do you think you're trying to prove?" I stammered in the face of his anger, confused by his questions, completely unable to manage an intelligent response. The more I stuttered, the angrier he became. Finally, he blew up, leaping out of his chair, overturning it in fury. I sat frozen, searching my brain for something to say, too frightened by then to say anything. After raging at me for another minute, he turned on his heel and stomped angrily out of sight. I just sat there, staring at my plate, my mind numb, praying for the meal to be over.

Just as I'd begun to hope he wasn't coming back, Mr. Rawlinson returned. Resuming his seat at the head of the table, Mr. Rawlinson stared at his own glass, then looked up at us. His glass was only about a third full. Every one of us knew we were in for trouble; we'd already been warned to keep his glass more than half full at all times. We had been so distracted by Mr. Rawlinson's explosion that we'd forgotten to refill it. He glared at each of us, one by one. Then, barely taking his eyes off us, he flipped his partially empty glass upside down on the table without spilling a drop. The gesture was so quick that none of us saw how he did it. We all stared at the table. There sat the glass, upside down, in front of him, the red liquid still trapped inside. Turning to me with his cold eyes, he ordered, "Mace, fill my glass. It's nearly empty."

I had no idea what to do next. I glanced at my fellow knobs, hoping for help. One or two peered at me from the corners of their eyes, looking as helpless as I felt, but the others kept their eyes straight ahead. Everyone at that table knew that I'd just been ordered to do the impossible. If I lifted the glass to refill it, the vacuum would be broken and the red stuff would rush out, spilling onto Mr. Rawlinson's clean trousers. Yet, I couldn't ignore a direct order. At last I requested permission to rise and, clutching my napkin in my hand, moved toward the head of the table.

With sweat running into my eyes, I rolled the napkin up, placed it by the edge of the glass facing Mr. Rawlinson, and took a deep breath. Screwing up all my nerve, I flipped the glass upright as quickly as I could and dove to catch the escaping liquid with the rolled napkin. The red stain moved steadily toward the edge of the table and Mr. Rawlinson's trousers, but I managed to reach it with my napkin before it spilled over the edge. Requesting extra napkins from the other knobs, I mopped up the spilled liquid, wiped the outside of Mr. Rawlinson's glass clean, and refilled it to the brim with red stuff. The entire time I worked Mr.

Rawlinson racked me for my clumsiness. My only comfort was that it could have been much worse. I could have dumped the stuff right onto Mr. Rawlinson's trousers. I didn't even want to think about what might have happened then. Just as I requested permission to return to my seat, the mess period came to an end, and I was dismissed with the rest of the Band Company knobs.

Marching was next—hour after hour of endless marching under the glaring sun. We began with drills in the barracks and soon moved outside onto the grass of the Parade Field, blinding in the August light. As a member of Band Company, I had to carry my clarinet in formation, learning to handle it smoothly without losing focus on my military bearing. Time after time, I was pulled out of line to be instructed in how to stand, how to hold the instrument, how to position my free arm. Some cadets got dizzy and had to sit down; others were taken to the infirmary as the afternoon wore on toward evening. My dark T-shirt stuck to my back, and for the first time I was grateful that my newly shaven neck was bare. I could feel the first pricking of sunburn where the razor had trimmed off the hair. Every half hour our cadre would stop us, have us stand at Parade rest, and make us take a long pull of water from the canteens we wore on the backs of our belts. Moving from knob to knob, they would check our water supply and make certain we weren't showing signs of heat stroke before we resumed drilling. Finally, after what seemed an eternity of strutting and rhythmic noise, we were marched back to the barracks.

Once in our quarters, our exhausted little platoon of freshmen changed out of our soaked PTs and into our duty uniforms. It was only then that the joyous truth began to filter into my brain. As I slicked back my short wet hair, the feel of my skull unfamiliar under my fingers, I looked down at the trousers I had so carefully adjusted. For the first time in 153 years of Citadel history, a woman was wearing the gray striped trousers of The South Carolina Corps of Cadets.

At 1800 hours, standing in formation with 576 of my classmates, all the exhaustion and stress of the day seemed to fall away from me. A light summer rain began to fall, cooling the grass and bathing the Parade grounds in a soft shimmer. My skin drank in the coolness. I could hear the media cameras snapping and whirring all around, but they didn't matter. From a podium yards in front of me, Cadet Colonel Butler ordered us to raise our hands and repeat after him. Everything but my fellow cadets dimmed into the background as I began to recite the oath that would both tie me to the path and connect me to the future:

I, Nancy Ruth Mace, hereby engage to serve as a cadet in The Citadel, The Military College of South Carolina, until graduation, or, until I shall be discharged by proper authority, and I promise to support loyally the constituted authorities thereof as long as I remain a member of the Corps of Cadets. I certify that I am not married.

Unfortunately, my moment of glory was short-lived. We still had dinner mess ahead of us. I was too tired and hot to want food, and I knew that dinner meant another miserable ordeal in a stuffy, noisy room. That evening we had to recite the first of our "Mess Facts." We were required to recite memorized information twice a day, at lunch and dinner, every single weekday from August to May during freshman year. We were expected to learn dozens of pages from the *Guidons* we carried around our necks in our idiot bags every waking hour. The basic list of requirements was called "Knob Knowledge" and included thirteen items:

1. The Citadel *Alma Mater*
2. All buildings on campus (their names, locations, and significance)
3. The Cadet Prayer
4. All Cadet Ranks and Insignias
5. The Cadet TO&E (Table of Organization and Equipment)
6. Presidents, dates, and services
7. All Guard Orders
8. The Definition of Hazing
9. The Honor Code
10. Cadet Language and Definitions
11. Mess Facts
12. The Definition of Sexual Harassment
13. The Significance of The Citadel Ring

Most of the items, such as the Prayer and the Creed, were fairly straightforward. Others were even funny. (WHAT DO KNOBS OUT-RANK? Sir, the president's cat, the commandant's dog, and all the captains at VMI, sir!) Even our official reason for coming to the Mess Hall was funny. (WHY DO KNOBS COME TO THE MESS HALL? Sir, three times a day and even more often, the highly esteemed upperclass cadets of this, our beloved institution, discover that their gastric juices are running wild and their large intestines are craving victuals. It is altogether fitting and proper, as well as obvious and natural, that it behooves the lowly plebe to come to the Mess Hall in order to ensure that the upperclass are properly served, sir!)

Other elements, though, were walking nightmares to remember. Worried about the effects of my ADD, I had worked on the list all summer, but I was still scared to death I'd never remember it all. The building list, for example, included paragraphs on forty-three buildings, six major monuments, and a collection of smaller monuments, altogether comprising twenty-one pages in our *Guidons*. Worse yet, some of the definitions were hopelessly technical. (WHAT IS THE DEFINITION OF LEATHER? Sir, if the fresh skin of an animal, cleaned and divested of all hair, fat, and other extraneous matter, be submerged in a dilute solution of tannic acid, a chemical combination ensues; the gelatinous tissue of the skin is converted into a nonputrescible substance impervious to and insoluble in water. This, sir, is leather.) The TO&E included all twenty-three Cadet commanders, all rank-holders in our individual companies, the overall structure of the battalions (four battalions, four companies in each battalion, three platoons in each company, three squads in each platoon), and an endless list of cadet equipment. There were thirty-eight sleeve insignias (as I found out while getting racked in the Haze Maze), eighty-six Citadel terms, thirteen paragraph-long definitions, not to mention all of the history of the school we would learn. The night before, I'd spent over an hour carefully writing out Monday's Mess Facts over and over, painfully committing them to memory, yet I soon discovered it wasn't enough. Under the stress of that evening's nonstop racking, my mind went completely blank.

It's a wonder I managed to eat anything that night. I had no appetite for the nasty food in front of me, and pieces of Mess Facts kept spinning around and around in my head. I sat there on the front three inches of my chair, ramrod straight, my back the required nine inches from the chair back, and dutifully choked down the bland, greasy food with my chin tucked so far in that my throat would barely let the food pass. I could barely swallow, and it was only the first day. The only thing that made me feel any better was that the guys looked just as bad as I did. The important thing, I reassured myself, was that I had survived my first day.

There was no rock music to wake me the next morning, just the sound of reveille and cadet officers once again pounding on our doors. As I pulled myself out of my rack that second day, I winced. Every cell in my body hurt. Ready or not, my day had begun.

By 0600 I was jogging around the quad to join Band Company. Kim and the other women fell into place with Echo Company. All around me the darkened air was filled with the sounds of shouts as cadet officers issued a steady stream of orders. At 0610 we marched off to the Mess Hall. A rumor was already circulating in the ranks that the first freshman had quit.

My second day was a duplicate of the first, minus the haircut and the Haze Maze. The permanent exhaustion of knob year had already set in. By the time taps sounded at 2300 that night, I was too tired to worry about anything except getting a good night's sleep so I could do well on the next day's physical training test. The rumor was that the following night was the official Citadel Hell Night, described in such harrowing detail in Pat Conroy's *Lords of Discipline*. The cadre would neither confirm nor deny the rumor, but at that moment, I was too exhausted to care.

★ CHAPTER 5 ★

HELL NIGHT

The morning that ended in Hell Night began like the previous two, with reveille at 0500. By 0515 I was out on the Parade Field with the rest of my company. While I warmed up to the cadre's cadence of "One, one thousand; two, one thousand," bending and stretching on the damp grass, I ran my PT strategy through my head. I had to do well if I wanted the male cadets to take me seriously. I was confident but focused. When I'd set my original goals during the summer, I hadn't counted on being so tired by the time the test took place.

When we finished warming up, our squad sergeant stepped forward to speak to us. For once, he was encouraging. The PT test was the first of many obstacles that we would have to overcome if we hoped to become Citadel graduates, he reminded us, and for many cadets, it was the biggest challenge they had faced so far. The College policy for freshmen was very strict: Cadets who could not meet PT minimums would be given special training until they either met the standards or left the Corps. He rounded out his speech by telling us, "We're looking for a low-stress environment this morning. I don't want to see anyone quit out there. We believe you can all pass the PT tests if you make your best effort."

I knew there had been a lot of argument about the new PT standards for women. Eventually, Citadel administrators had decided to adopt the military training standard used for female recruits at West Point and the Army. The requirement was below the minimum for male recruits, but experts considered it equivalent for the female body. It would have been a challenge for most men. I wasn't worried about making the minimums. I'd been an athlete all my life, and I'd trained hard all summer for the test I was about to take. I wanted to "max out," earning the full 300 points awarded to cadets who made the maximum score on each test. There would be three of them: push-ups (eighteen for women, forty-two for men), sit-ups (fifty for women, fifty-two for men), each completed within a two-minute limit, and finally a two-mile run around campus, ending at the Parade ground (eighteen minutes for women, a little under sixteen minutes for men). As I stood among my classmates that morning, I felt my spirits rise for the first time in two days. I was going to kick some male butt this morning. I just knew it.

Just as the sun peeked over the horizon, we were divided into battalions and led across campus behind the Mess Hall to the grassy field lining the river. Clipboards in hand, the cadre began to put us through our paces. We started with push-ups. Twelve years of swimming and a summer of pumping myself off the ground paid off as my training officer counted aloud: thirty, forty, fifty push-ups, and a few more before time was called. So much for women only doing eighteen. Sit-ups were even better; I had curled my body off the ground well over fifty times by the end of two minutes. I was breathing hard, but I caught my breath quickly, my blood racing with excitement. Around me the other knobs from my company got to their feet. Most of them looked tired already. I watched one red-faced, chunky knob struggle for breath and wondered how on earth he had expected to survive Hell Week, much less first semester, without getting in shape first. We still had a two-mile run to go. By now the sun was up, and as I glanced over my shoulder, I could see the flash of cameras a few yards away. The press had arrived, telephoto lenses in hand, to watch us sweat.

I wasn't worried about finishing the run. I'd run every day all summer. My only concern was pacing myself so I could bring in a good time. I not only wanted to max out the female standard; I wanted to leave as many male knobs as possible in the dust. I had to do well. If I didn't, every sexist pig in the bunch would say the women couldn't cut it. I wanted to show them what a "girl" could do.

I showed them, all right. Several of the males couldn't finish the run, but every one of us women reached the finish line well within the required time. As I pounded down the last few hundred yards to the finish line at the Parade Field, I passed classmate after classmate, some of them already stumbling and gasping for air. I could hear my cadre shouting encouragement: "Go, knobby, go!" By the time I reached the finish, only three cadets were ahead of me. As I crossed the line, my training officers shouted, "Good job, knob, good job!" "Yo, Mace!" I felt like shouting in triumph. With a time of fifteen minutes, a full minute *under* the male standard, I was one of only four knobs in my company to pass all three PT tests. I felt wonderful. Behind me, hundreds of other freshmen still struggled to reach the finish. I cheered as Petra and Jeanie jogged by. Finally, we all marched away to breakfast, chanting, "They say that at The Citadel, the food is mighty fine." It was a huge lie, of course, and I struggled to keep from smiling. For the first time that week, I had done something right.

Unfortunately, my triumph of feminism was short-lived, for before the afternoon was over, I acted like a girl in the most embarrassing way. I burst into tears in front of my cadre. And all because of a picture in the local paper.

The funny thing was, the picture wasn't a problem for me. I'd known all summer that I'd be photographed constantly once school started; all us women would. What I hadn't thought about was the effect it would have on my classmates. The Monday before, as we waited to enter the Haze Maze, a photographer had snapped a picture of me. The whole row of us was standing at attention, memorizing pages out of the *Guidon*. The problem was that the photographer had not only gotten a picture of me; he'd also gotten a clear shot of the knob standing next to me, a classmate of mine named Maher. When the picture came out in the *Post and Courier* that Wednesday morning, there were the two of us, big as life in the frame. By the time I got back from lunch mess that day, the paper was circulating in the battalion. Drawing attention to yourself is fatal for a knob, and I already knew I would take considerable heat for the attention being focused on me. But instead of taking it out on me that day, the cadet sergeant took it out on Maher.

The minute we returned to the barracks after lunch mess the racking began. Shoving the newspaper into poor Maher's face as we stood in formation, the company clerks began to taunt him. "Hey, movie star! Showbiz knob! You think you're so cool, don't you, that you have to have your picture in the paper, don't you, smack!" Red-faced, Maher began to stutter out his response, "Sir, no, sir!", which was not the response the cadre wanted to hear. Immediately correcting himself, Maher sounded off, "Sir, yes, sir!", but this answer brought even more racking. By the time it occurred to Maher to reply, "Sir, no excuse, sir!", the cadre were screaming at the top of their lungs. I stood at attention a few feet away in mute misery, not daring to say a word in his defense for fear of making things worse. I knew that my classmate was being punished for something I had caused. I managed to hold back the tears, but by the time we were dismissed, I was shaking with emotion.

I didn't hold myself together for long. An hour later, as I jogged down the gallery toward the back sally port, Cadet Colonel Butler came up from behind, ordered me to halt, and whispered in my ear, "Who am I, smack? This is your triple diamond daddy. Tell me who I am." I blanked out completely and couldn't think of a thing to say. Worse, to my great embarrassment, I started to cry. Coming around in front of me, Mr. Butler immediately said, "What's wrong, Mace? Has something happened?"

I replied, "Sir, no sir. Sir, no excuse, sir," but I couldn't control my tears. With clear concern on his face, Mr. Butler continued to ask me what was wrong, and I repeated, "Sir, no excuse, sir," over and over as I cried. Finally, Mr. Butler put me in a nearby room and went in search of my platoon leader; a few minutes later, they both returned to speak with me. With genuine concern on their faces, they questioned me closely: Had anyone hurt me? Touched me inappropriately? Threatened me? Their unexpected concern only made me cry harder. After a minute or two of useless questioning, they gave up and just let me cry, which was undoubtedly the best thing they could have done under the circumstances. I sat down on the chair they offered me and cried myself out. Then, still sniffing back tears, I explained that my classmate was being racked unmercifully and that it was "all my fault" because of the picture in the paper. When I had talked it all out, they told me to stay put until I felt better and then rejoin the rest of my company. They would take care of the situation.

And they did. I later learned that the cadet involved was punished for his behavior. That day, though, I was just grateful for the care my commander had shown me. I had not expected that. I had learned a very important lesson: that my cadre might challenge, even torment me, but when it really mattered, they were on my side. They would not let anyone hurt the knobs under their command. When I fell in with the rest of my company an hour later, my face washed clean of any trace of tears, I felt my first sense of connection with the cadet officers who intimidated me so much. After all, we were in this together.

Wednesday had already been the most exhausting day I had endured so far. After doing PT tests at dawn, bursting into tears after lunch, and drilling for long hours in the hot Charleston sun, I longed for rest and quiet. That, of course, was out of the question. That night was Hell Night, easily the most traumatic event any knob experiences at The Citadel. To use the politically correct term, Hell Night is when many freshmen "rethink their decision" to be members of the Corps. It is an intense combination of intimidation, initiation, and high drama. No one who survives that evening ever forgets it.

I returned from evening mess to wait nervously for dusk. Rumors were running through the barracks that tonight would be Hell Night, but no one was certain. We would have to wait and see what darkness held. My body was already aching with exhaustion, but no amount of physical fatigue could relieve the tension that built steadily in the battalion as the sun set and the barracks began to darken. Like every other knob in the College that night, Kim and I had been ordered to dress in PTs and then confined to quarters. We passed the time shining our brass and whispering nervously. After the noise and chaos of the day, the hush that lay over the barracks felt unnatural. The checkered quad lay silent, and the distant crackle of media cameras outside the battalion walls seemed a world away. At 2000 we were ordered to go to bed, just as if it were any other night. No one put on pajamas. Instead, still wearing PTs, we crawled beneath the covers, and waited.

Shortly afterward, the heavy iron gates of all the barracks clanged shut, locking us inside, and a large blue tarp was carefully draped over each sally port to block the prying gaze of the media. We could no longer get out, and they could no longer see in. Like the sign that supposedly hangs over the front gates of hell, the unspoken message that echoed through the corridors of Padgett–Thomas Barracks was "No escape." I waited in the silence with my roommate, filled with a mixture of anxiety and excitement. This would be my first major test of nerve and commitment, and I was determined not to fail.

At exactly 2100, the silence was shattered by the sound of the cadre pounding on our doors, ordering us into the quad at once. All hell began to break loose.

In the heat and the darkness, a hundred or more knobs raced to take their assigned places on the red and white squares under the galleries.

Out the door and to the left, Kim raced to take her place with Echo Company while I ran to take my place with Band. Four companies of knobs besides my own occupied my barracks, and I dimly glimpsed the knobs from Echo Company, F-Troop, Golf, and Hotel taking their places in the four corners of the quad as I joined my own formation. As we all snapped to attention, I could see little beyond the white athletic shoes and socks of my classmates glinting in the darkness. Each knob was called out and placed individually on a red square of the quad. Much like a checkerboard, we were all spaced out so the cadre could surround us later on. Once in place, I about-faced on order and looked into the cavern of shadows behind us. Everything was dark, from the athletic clothing we all wore to the navy blue tarp barely visible behind the gates in front of me.

When the last knob scrambled into place, utter silence descended. As the seconds ticked into agonizing minutes, sweat trickled down my neck and between my shoulder blades. The steamy South Carolina air seemed to thicken in my lungs, a warm and tangible darkness that became claustrophobic as the silence deepened. I started to feel like anything was better than this endless waiting.

After what could not have been more than two or three minutes, a voice rang out. All eyes were immediately riveted on the source of that voice. Above us on the second gallery stood the Band Company commander. All five company commanders had silently taken their places in the darkness above their knobs, positioned precisely in all four corners and the exact middle of the second gallery, about ten feet above our heads. Each commander began speaking at the identical moment to his small company of knobs, trembling in the shadows below him. The commander of Band Company, Mr. Thaxton, stood directly above me. He spoke to us of the Fourth Class System, of a century of Citadel tradition, of what it means to become a member of The South Carolina Corps of Cadets. He told us what it means to spend nine months of your life as a knob, the lowest link in The Citadel food chain. Somehow, in the darkness above us, each word the commanders spoke became heavy with significance. We drank in every syllable. There weren't many. Less than three minutes after they had begun speaking, they issued their final instruction: "Knobs, close your eyes, and remain at attention!" As my lids dropped obediently, silence descended once again, and the waiting resumed. The sweat trickled into my ears, and I could hear nothing beyond the ragged breathing of my classmates and the pounding of my own heart. The only words that would form in my mind as I tried to reassure myself were "Oh, shit. Oh, shit. This is going to be bad."

I could neither see nor hear them, but into the silence around us, the cadre had begun to filter, stealthy as death. Sensing their presence, the hair on the back of my neck began to rise. After what seemed another eternity, the order rang out, "Open your eyes, knobs!" As I did, I was startled to find that the cadre had surrounded us, their sudden nearness a shock to my senses. They were deployed in two lines, half having entered from the right, half from the left, meeting in the middle to form a V, the two lines facing each other at the apex. Deadly silent, they stood unmoving. Their covers were pulled down over their eyes, and as I stared at their rigid muscular bodies, I thought that they seemed more like robots than human beings.

The illusion got stronger a moment later when Mr. Thaxton began to introduce the members of our cadre. The silent V now faced us, a row of identical figures in gray uniforms, their brims pulled down and their heads bowed at Parade rest. I already knew most of them by name, but in the unnatural silence, they seemed ghostly and unfamiliar. As each man's name rang out, he stepped smartly forward—left foot, right foot, in sharp staccato rhythm—popped his head up, then reversed the ritual: head down, right foot back, left foot back, Parade rest. Cadet after cadet repeated the sequence, a long robotic line of such precision that none of the cadre seemed to be flesh and bone, only cold gray metal. With their eyes invisible under the brims of their covers, there was nothing human about them. Finally, reaching the end of the line, he introduced the two sophomore clerks and barked out the order, "Post!" The two company clerks who formed the terminal points of the V, nearest the knobs, suddenly ran screaming toward us. Just as suddenly they braced, one facing front and the other side, only inches from our faces. Startled, I stifled an urge to scream. Only when the last cadet had snapped back into place did Mr. Thaxton speak again.

From that night on, he told us, we were members of The Citadel's Fourth Class and were expected to behave accordingly. We were to brace on command, he told us, gesturing toward the two rigid figures who modeled the position for us. A braced knob was to stand rigidly at attention, palms at a forty-five-degree angle to the body, fists parallel to the dark stripe of our uniform trousers, shoulders rolled back and down, chin and forehead pulled back so tightly that folds of flesh emerged under our chins. If an upperclass cadet entered our room, he informed us, we were to call the room to attention and brace until the cadet left the room. During mealtimes in the Mess Hall, we were to brace at all times, either in the standing position or perched on our chairs as we ate.

Furthermore, Mr. Thaxton informed us, we were to brace anytime we were outside of our rooms in the barracks. We were to run everywhere we went within the confines of the barracks, always braced, even when running up stairs. Running in a braced position meant keeping our elbows locked, our forearms parallel to the ground, our chins tucked tightly into that impossibly painful position. And finally, we were told, every step we took outside of our barracks must be with eyes straight ahead, moving at the rate of 120 steps per minute as we rushed down the gutters between the battalions of the College, for walking on sidewalks or across open areas was a privilege reserved for upperclassmen.

When Mr. Thaxton's instructions came to an end, we were once more told to close our eyes. As my eyes fluttered shut, another voice began to emerge over the college-wide loudspeaker. The voice was that of Cadet Colonel Butler. He began to speak to us of the solemnity of the hours that lay before us, and as he did so, ever so imperceptibly at first, the poignant notes of a harmonica crept into the background. As Mr. Butler continued to speak, the harmonica grew louder until it nearly—but not quite—drowned out his voice. I gradually became aware that the melody being played was "Home, Sweet Home," and in the stillness and anxiety of the moment, my heart suspended in time, the familiar notes took on a haunting quality. Words and melody blended into a harmony of fear. As I listened in that harmonic silence, I felt a movement nearby—a stealthy sense of bodies moving into place among us. Involuntarily, I shivered.

Finally, as the last note of the harmonica faded, Mr. Butler solemnly announced, "The Fourth Class System is now in effect."

With Mr. Butler's last word, Mr. Thaxton abruptly barked out the order: "Open your eyes! Brace, knobs!" As I struggled to pull my body into the unnatural position, I was aware of rapid movement all around me. A few seconds later, in response to another shouted order—"Open your eyes, knobs!"—I found myself face-to-face with the menacing presence of a cadet officer, and hell began.

In the overpowering chaos that followed, the silence of the last hour was jerked out from under us. All at once, the cadre was on us, moving from knob to knob with long, monsterlike steps, screaming obscenities in our faces. "Brace, knob! I told you to brace!" was screamed in our ears from inches away, deafening us with pain. Their eyes remained veiled as they racked us, spit flying, the smell of sweat assaulting our nostrils, fury burning in the eyeless darkness beneath their brims. They moved from one to another of us, screaming orders in our faces at impossible rates, ordering us to march, to brace, to pop off, all the while making it impossible for us to do any of it properly. For what seemed an eternity, I marched, I shouted jumbled pieces of required information, I felt their hot breath and heard their screaming obscenities. "Brace, shitbag! Chin back, smack!" I struggled to force my body into the inhuman posture as my spine resisted. I could feel the sweat soaking every centimeter of my body, and only the adrenaline pumping through my veins kept me on my feet. They say that hell is filled with the screams of the damned. This was close enough for me.

Nearly two hours went by. It might as well have been an eternity. Finally, one by one, we were dismissed and sent running to the showers.

As I jogged wearily around the quad toward my room, I heard a voice shout, "Halt, Mace!" I stopped and snapped to attention, struggling to force my exhausted body into one last brace. In the shadows under the corner stairwell, where no one else in the barracks could see him, stood Mr. Wizeman, the operations sergeant who had told me the week before that I was unwelcome at The Citadel. I swallowed hard, wondering what was coming next. "Sir, yes, sir!" I managed to force out.

Mr. Wizeman stepped a little closer, and as he did, his serious face came into my line of vision. He spoke clearly, but quietly. "Mace, you must promise me that you will never quit and that I will see you graduate from The Citadel with my own eyes. Do you understand me, knob?"

I understood. I couldn't believe what I was hearing. Little tears formed in the corners of my eyes as I replied, "Sir, yes, sir!" Mr. Wizeman was not offering me his friendship, for that would come much later, but he was offering me something much more valuable: his respect. Quietly, Mr. Wizeman dismissed me, and I sprinted to my room.

As I jogged the remaining yards to my room, my heart soared. As I wearily entered my room, the adrenaline began to seep away, and I could feel the pain in my body. In spite of the pain, a blessed sense of relief began sinking in, for I knew the worst was over. I had done it. I peeled off my sweat-drenched clothing, grabbed my robe and towel, and raced back down the gallery toward the women's showers. The confusion in the battalion had begun to lessen. I was vaguely aware that Petra and Kim were right behind me, but there was neither time nor breath for contact. Turning on the shower head full-blast, I stood trembling with fatigue and washed off the sweat. Less than a minute later, before I had even finished soaping, I could hear pounding on our shower room door and a cadet roaring, "Get the hell out of out there, Mace! What do you think this is, a spa?" Within seconds I had turned off the water, wrapped my terry cloth robe hastily around me, and raced out the door toward my room, the damp towel still clutched in my hands. Another sixty seconds of door pounding and racking brought me out of my quarters again, dressed in clean PTs, to join the company lineup for the nightly blister check. Once my feet were examined, I was dismissed for lights-out.

It was over. I had survived. I glanced at my watch. Less than two hours had passed. Incredible. It seemed like a lifetime.

In surviving Hell Night, I had won my first major battle. From that moment on, I would never look back. No matter what lay ahead, I was determined that Mr. Wizeman—and my father—would watch me walk across the fieldhouse stage one day and receive my diploma.

★ CHAPTER 6 ★

SURVIVOR

Thursday morning I awoke to a whole new world. The Fourth Class System had officially begun, and until Recognition Day nine long months away, I was at the mercy of every upperclass cadet on campus. Saturday was our last day alone with our cadre; Sunday would bring the rest of the Corps, hundreds of them, all of them outranking me. Worse yet, knob rules were now in full force, for from now on, I would be expected to run, brace, or both every time I left my room. And that wasn't even counting the classes that started in three days. How was I going to study and deal with ADD when I was already too tired to think by sundown?

Still, I managed to hold onto my sense of humor. Thursday brought one of many funny incidents that came to symbolize, at least for me, the real changes that were taking place at The Citadel. For the first time in the history of the Corps, a cadet started a menstrual period. In fact, all four of us did, all within an hour of each other. If that didn't prove we had a unified spirit, I don't know what would have. Everything considered, the whole incident was pretty funny.

It began in the infirmary, where Mr. Acevedo had taken me for a blister check. Three days of marching in leather shoes had left my feet covered with watery blisters. They had to be treated to prevent infection. While the nurse was treating my feet, I discovered that my period had started. I was very surprised, for it wasn't due for another two weeks. "Figures," I thought, "just another day in Hell Week. Lucky me. Nothing like being racked with PMS."

Once my blisters had been cleaned and covered with Nuskin, I faced the embarrassing task of explaining my problem to Mr. Acevedo. I needed to get back to my quarters, to find my tampons, and to shower and change before rejoining my company. I told Mr. Acevedo as matter-of-factly as possible that I had a "female problem" and needed to go back to the battalion to take care of it. He looked at me blankly, his smooth brown face expressionless. Clearly, he had no idea what I was talking about. After a moment of awkward silence, I told him bluntly that my period had started, that I had no tampons, and that I needed to go back to the barracks immediately. That, he understood. For the first time that week, one of my cadre was more uncomfortable than I was. A tampon emergency was clearly outside his range of experience.

He agreed hurriedly, looking away from me, then rushed me back to my quarters as fast as he could. As we neared the door to my quarters, I saw that Mr. Wizeman had organized a "Shine Detail" right on the front stoop, where my platoon of knobs now sat, industriously polishing their brass buckles. "Oh, great," I thought, and apparently so did Mr. Acevedo. He looked upset and ordered me to hurry up and "take care of business," then confine myself to quarters until I was ordered to rejoin my company. Clearly puzzled, Mr. Wizeman asked Mr. Acevedo what was going on. As Mr. Acevedo took him aside for a whispered conference, I dodged into my room, stepping over a fellow knob to do so, slammed the door, and locked it.

Red-faced, I grabbed clean underwear, a tampon, and a towel, stuffed the tampon and underwear under my shirt where no one could see them, unlocked the door, stepped over the knobs, and raced to the showers. A couple of them glanced up at me curiously but said nothing. Rinsing myself quickly off in the shower room, I changed into clean PTs, bundled my bloodstained clothing in the towel, and ran back to my room as fast as I could. Once there, I stuffed the dirty clothes deep into my laundry bag, grabbed my shine kit, and tried to join the shine party on my stoop. The minute I sat down both Mr. Acevedo and Mr. Wizeman shouted at me to go back in my room, lock the door, and stay there until they told me to come out. I sat on my rack for what felt like forever, not knowing whether to laugh or cry.

Finally, the Human Affairs cadet officer arrived to interview me about my "incident." He asked if I needed to go to the infirmary, to be excused from drilling, to have medication or special supplies. I could see that he was trying to be thoughtful and supportive, and I appreciated it. I explained that I was fine, that I'd just needed to wash off and get my tampons before going back to my company. I also told him that my cramps were mild, that as an athlete I was used to dealing with them, and that a couple of Tylenol were usually enough to make me comfortable. Finally, I asked to rejoin my company for the rest of the day, telling him that I would let my squad sergeant know if there was a problem.

Satisfied, he dismissed me to my platoon. Heaving a sigh of relief, I went to rejoin my company. The whole mess was beginning to strike me as funny. The next time a cadet began menstruating, I hoped, everyone would be less hysterical about it.

It wasn't until the evening that I found out how bizarre the timing of my period had been. Kim had also started her period that morning, shortly before I did. We soon learned that Petra and Jeanie had started that day, too, also ahead of schedule, in a strange sort of sympathetic bonding among the four of us. The Corps talks continually about brotherhood among cadets. Obviously, we were well on our way to sisterhood.

Friday was a duplicate of Thursday, except for the excitement over my period. By Sunday morning, five freshmen had dropped out, less than usual for Hell Week. After five days of hell, we were looking forward to Saturday, but it brought little relief. We continued to drill in our duty uniforms, and Band Company practiced long hours on the Parade Field. Our "free" hours were spent studying and working our uniforms. We didn't dare go to sleep.

My parents attended Summerall Chapel again that Sunday morning, and once again I was not allowed to speak with them. Still, it felt good knowing they were there. Services that day would be followed by the annual beach party for freshmen, held at the College Beach House on the Isle of Palms, about twenty miles from the main campus. For the first time since my arrival, I would be alone with College officials and my classmates for a few hours, without the cadre watching my every move. No cadet officers, just food and the ocean and a chance to loaf around and sleep. It sounded like heaven. I felt a stab of homesickness as I caught sight of my mother out of the corner of my eye, but by the time I boarded the bus for the beach trip two hours later, I was feeling pretty good.

It was a beautiful afternoon as I rode with my company down the narrow streets of Sullivan's Island, en route to the Isle of Palms. Looking out the window, I could see that the neighborhood had been almost completely rebuilt since the destruction of Hurricane Hugo seven years before. The wind was rising outside our bus, but there was no sign of a storm, just some blessed relief from the heavy heat. Scattered among the clapboard beach houses were the locally famous "hill houses," round structures built partially underground for protection from the storms. Their odd colors and globelike shapes reminded me of alien dwellings I had seen in science fiction movies. We talked quietly as the bus rounded the curves. We had a whole day of relaxation ahead of us, starting with hamburgers and hot dogs at 1300 and ending with the ride home at 1830, shortly before dusk. It would be a long time before we had such freedom again, and I intended to enjoy it while I could.

And I did. After stuffing myself on picnic food on the lawn overlooking the ocean, I walked down to the beach alone for some precious time to myself. It felt wonderful to kick off my sneakers and sink my toes in the damp sand, my blisters giving a sigh of relief as the sand soothed them. Lying back against the tidal reef of sand, I stretched every muscle in my aching body. Rubbing the muscles in my neck, sore and rigid from days of bracing in that impossibly unnatural position, I closed my eyes and lifted my face to the sun. The salt air gently caressed me, and I breathed it deeply into my lungs. The shouts and laughter of my fellow knobs, nearly fifty yards behind me, faded into the background. It felt good to be alive, wonderful to have survived my week of hell. I smiled to myself. One week down and a couple hundred to go.

After dozing happily for a few minutes, I pulled the paper and pen I had brought with me out of my satchel and balanced the tablet on my knees to write. The cadre had ordered all freshmen to write letters home, telling our families what wonderful fun Hell Week had been. There had been no time for more than a dropped line since Hell Week had begun, seven days and a lifetime ago, and freshmen were not allowed to call home for another month. One by one, I wanted to connect with my whole family, beginning with a long letter to my parents and then another one to my brother. I still checked my mail every evening, hoping for a letter from home. None had come so far, but they knew how busy I was. And there was so much I wanted to tell them.

I had finished my first letter and was just beginning a letter to James when I thought I heard a familiar voice on the breeze. That was odd. I would have sworn I'd heard my mother's voice. "I must be hallucinating," I thought. Glancing around, I returned to my writing, but a few minutes later I heard an exclaimed, "There she is!" followed immediately by a male voice saying to shush. This was definitely not my imagination. Sitting up, I saw my mother, James, and my sister Beth Ann rounding the corner of a sand dune, walking along the water's edge toward me. I couldn't believe my eyes. Holding out her arms, my mother dropped beside me and enveloped me in a startled embrace as I stammered, "What are you doing here? You know it's against the rules!"

"I know, but I just had to see you for a minute to make sure you were all right," she told me, looking earnestly into my face.

Laughing, Beth Ann said, "You know Mom. There's no stopping her when she gets an idea in her head," and I was hugged by my sister and brother. Sure enough, my mom had decided to walk in the back way in hopes of getting a minute with me. Torn between joy and the fear of getting caught, I didn't know whether to thank her or throttle her. Instead, I babbled a few quick reassurances, told them I'd just been writing them letters, and warned that they'd better get out of there before we got caught. Fortunately, her mission accomplished, my mother knew enough to beat a hasty retreat. Watching their backs disappear back down the beach, I laughed. I didn't need to worry. They were definitely thinking about me.

The sun hung low over the horizon as we boarded the bus to return to campus that evening. The ride back was far more silent than the one out, for we were all tired from the long week behind us, and sobered by the thought of the following day. I had to struggle to keep the old anxiety out of my head as I thought about the coming days. When the bus pulled back through the campus gates, I felt even worse.

While the freshmen had been relaxing at the Beach House, the remainder of the Corps had been returning, for academic classes started on Wednesday. We filed off the bus under the hostile stare of hundreds of upperclassmen, newly arrived and dressed in their uniforms. Up until then, the only cadets on campus had been knobs and cadre. The cadre might be hard on us, but they were also there to protect and teach us, for they wanted their company to shine. These other cadets had no interest in either helping or protecting us; to them, we were just nameless faces, a ready-made slave class who would have to obey their every command. Instead of worrying about pleasing a couple hundred cadets, we would now have to satisfy a couple thousand upperclass cadets. It was hard not to feel outnumbered. We were. We were also completely intimidated.

School was starting, beginning with my first class at 0800 on Wednesday. Push had come to shove. It was only three taps and three reveilles away.

CHAPTER 7

STORMY WEATHER

Several weeks usually go by before freshmen are allowed into the world beyond The Citadel's iron walls. In my case, however, fate intervened far sooner than that. Two days after the beach party, a hurricane threatened South Carolina, with the eye of the storm expected to come ashore at Charleston. With the campus only a stone's throw from the Atlantic, even The Citadel wasn't prepared to argue with Mother Nature.

During the second week of September, a bed-down/evacuation was called for the Corps of Cadets, with all cadets within driving distance of home released to their families. Since my family lived less than thirty miles from campus, I found myself hurriedly battening down the barracks, packing up my belongings, and joining other cadets in my company outside the battalion gates to wait for my ride home. I was taking two of my Band Company classmates, Ryan and Mike, with me. Too far away to evacuate to their own homes, they had been more than happy to accept my parents' invitation to take refuge at my house and eat some home cooking.

Nearly all twenty-four Band Company knobs had gathered just outside the front sally port, chatting and watching the cloud-filled sky as we waited for our transportation to arrive. While we waited, Colonel Trez came by to say a few words of encouragement about the hurricane. We all came to attention at his approach, but he immediately told us to sit down and be comfortable, asking us a few questions to make sure we had a safe place to go. After a minute or two, he moved on.

Almost immediately the 2nd battalion commander, Mr. Jones, came over to speak with us. He had been watching our conversation with the colonel, and as he drew close to our group, he motioned me aside to speak with me privately. I could tell by his expression that he was furious, but I had no idea why.

Without any warning, he began speaking to me with intense anger. "I don't care whether or not you know Colonel Trez through your family! I still expect you to treat the colonel in a respectful manner." Surprised and embarrassed, I felt my mind racing. What was he talking about? I didn't know Colonel Trez through my family.

He continued, "It is common courtesy and simple respect to stand when an officer addresses you." Flushing, I could feel my eyes begin to water as he went on. "I know your father is a general himself, but that is no excuse. You should know better than anyone that an officer is to be treated with respect."

I stammered, "Sir, yes, sir," then requested permission to explain. I told Mr. Jones that we had all come to attention for Colonel Trez, but that the colonel had insisted we all sit down again while he spoke with us. Mr. Jones was not impressed with my explanation, telling me I was a "gaudy little smack." I swallowed back resentment as he walked away, vowing to myself never to make that same mistake again.

I felt terrible, for I had been taught since I was a little girl to show proper respect to a superior officer. At the same time, I was angry about the way Mr. Jones had singled me out. Nearly twenty of us had been part of the conversation with Colonel Trez, yet Mr. Jones chose to rack only me. He had not said a word to my male classmates. I did not believe it was a coincidence.

Twenty minutes later, all my misery faded away as my father pulled up in the blue Cadillac, and I rushed to meet him. For the first time in over two weeks, I was able to hug my dad, and it had never felt better. After introducing Ryan and Mike, we stowed our gear in the trunk and piled into the car. We laughed all the way home, sharing ridiculous stories about the cadre and our bonehead classmates. In the safety and comfort of my father's car, all the stress of the last two weeks faded away, and everything that had happened began to seem funny. My dad didn't say much, but every now and then I could see his cigar quiver as he chuckled, and I remembered all the stories he had once told me about his own days as a cadet. I suddenly felt wonderful. I loved The Citadel. Going there was the best decision I had ever made.

That night, in the comfort of my old bed, I slept like a baby for eleven hours straight and woke to find my mother making French toast. The sky had cleared. It looked like Hurricane Fran was going to bypass us after all. Life was good.

The time at home passed happily, but after the first twenty-four hours, I found myself getting nervous. The sudden change from Hell Week to home had thrown off my physical and psychological rhythm, and I felt myself tensing up at the thought of returning to school. Part of me could hardly wait to get back to campus, but another part of me felt the seductive pull of home, sleep, food, and comfort. I found myself picking quarrels with my mother, restless and ambivalent about the state of limbo Fran had forced me into. When my classmates and I returned to campus in time for classes on Monday, I didn't know whether I felt more anxiety or relief.

Classes began immediately. Everybody who has heard of the Corps knows about the marching, the haircuts, the push-ups, the physical demands of cadet life. What most people forget, however, is that The Citadel is a college, and college means academics. Knob year is not boot camp; it is *college* with boot camp, and the administration never lets you forget it. From the moment you check into the barracks and attend your first orientation meeting as a freshman, you are continually reminded that academics are the first priority at The Citadel. That reality hit me in the face when I returned from my brief visit home.

It took all my determination to convince myself that I could cope with academics and military life at the same time. I'd worked hard to overcome my ADD, but on the night before classes resumed, all the old anxiety came flooding back. What if I couldn't do this after all? The goal I'd set for myself was straight A's, a perfect 4.0. I took deep breaths and tried to focus. "You can do this, you can do this," I told myself over and over as I finally drifted off to sleep.

The academic schedule I had chosen for myself was intimidating: ROTC, biology, accounting, math, calculus, English, and health. By the time the first day was over, I knew I had bitten off more than I could chew, and I dropped one of the math classes. Calculus, I decided, was more than enough.

Coping with my courses also meant documenting my learning disability with the college. As much as I disliked being labeled as an "LD" student, the reality was that I would not survive academically unless I had the support of Student Services. I filled out the necessary paperwork and arranged to have my doctors' evaluations sent to Dr. Zaremba, the head of Support Services. I also received permission to continue with my ADD medication, which was essential to my survival.

With the required paperwork and support services in place, the rest was up to me. Hoping to get off to a good start, I made the first of many trips to the Cadet Store for school supplies, purchasing several packages of three-by-five cards to organize my class and textbook notes. In the following days I added to my organizational system, purchasing colored folders and organizers for my desk drawers to help keep my notes and materials orderly. I was determined to be the most organized knob in my company, for I knew that was the only way I could keep a handle on all the challenges I was facing. I refused to think about failing. Every time the thought arose, I pushed it out. One way or another, I was going to do this.

I pushed myself hard, driven by a need to succeed that made little sense to some of the other freshmen. From the very first day of classes, I spent my Evening Study Period (ESP) poring over my books and notes, taking time out only to do calisthenics and work on my Mess Facts. I rarely gave myself a break. It took me longer than most people to memorize, and I usually had to work past lights out to get everything completed. Only the interruptions of battalion life, like shine parties and other knob duties, cut into the hours I had set aside to study. The fear of failing haunted me; I could not afford to blow this opportunity. I would do whatever was necessary to make sure I did not.

It wasn't easy. Nothing in those early weeks was easy. Classes were stressful, for I had to deal with psychological as well as academic challenges every time I slid into my desk chair. I found myself isolated and estranged in class. From the first day I sat down in a classroom, I was alone. Jeanie was in my English class, but I sat in the front row where I could tune out distractions, whereas she usually came late and sat in the back by the door. No one would sit with me, or even near me for that matter. The area around me was a small island of isolation, my desk surrounded by empty chairs. Sometimes my classmates whispered comments under their breath. More often they simply ignored me, as if I was invisible. I tried not to let them see how much it hurt. It was high school all over again.

The teachers did not treat me differently because I was a female; in fact, for the first few classes, one of my professors called me "Mr. Mace." I was pretty sure he didn't mean to insult me; if anything, he called me "Mr." out of habit. It made me uncomfortable, but I couldn't very well correct him. Addressed as a male, yet ignored as a female, the hours I spent in class were awkward and lonely.

With all their demands, academic classes were only a small part of my day. I was required to follow a detailed "Cadet 24-Hour Schedule" for freshmen, which the school told us would "contribute to the intense, high-stress nature of the Fourth Class System." As if we needed more stress. From the day we returned from Fran Furlough, every minute of our time was lived according to a strict set of rules.

There were two schedules: Weekday and Weekend. The Weekday Schedule applied to Mondays through Thursdays. With few variations, it followed the same pattern. At 0500 reveille sounded, courtesy of my classmates in Band Company, and the barracks gates were unlocked. By 0615 we had to report to the platoon sergeant on the gallery, ready for "Sweep Detail." At 0645 we would be sent to put away our brooms. Someone inevitably wiped out my shoes during Sweep Detail, and I soon learned to have a second pair polished and ready, to change into before reporting back to formation. Sick call was next, with cadet officers responsible for sending sick freshmen to the infirmary to be checked over.

Shortly after 0700, we would reassemble in formation, and by 0720 we would be marching to breakfast mess. After breakfast and the day's announcements, we had fifteen minutes to return to our quarters and prepare for class. A trumpet called us to class at 0750 (there were trumpet calls, called "steel," at ten minutes before the hour all morning and afternoon, to order us to the next activity).

From 0800 to 1150 on Monday, Wednesday, and Friday, we were in class, three fifty-minute classes scheduled like any other college student's, except we went in uniform and listened for bugles instead of bells. On Tuesday and Thursday however, at 1100 we assembled with our company in the Band Hall for an hour's drill. Then 1210 brought formal inspection in the battalion, braced and toeing the line. We rushed to our rooms to prepare for inspection, then met in the squad room to look each other over and make sure everyone looked all right. Punishment would be assigned if anyone's appearance wasn't perfect. It wasn't enough to get it right myself; we were judged as a team. One of the knobs in my platoon was always forgetting his belt. It drove us all crazy.

At 1220 there was the march to lunch mess, where we would spend fifteen minutes on the edge of our chairs trying to brace, eat, and pop off Mess Facts, all at the same time. After our dismissal back to the barracks, we were given a few minutes to listen to company announcements and gather up our books and homework before the next class call at 1250. Then it was classes for another three hours, followed by one hour of physical training on Mondays and Wednesdays. Tuesdays and Thursdays were for intramural sports, and drill at 1100, also required for freshmen. Afternoons (on Wednesday, Friday, and Saturday) were also the time when unlucky cadets walked their punishment tours and sat confinements, The Citadel equivalent of detention.

At 1815 there was another call and formation to assemble, followed by the supper march to the Mess Hall for another fifteen minutes of bad food, stiff posture, and Mess Facts, always accompanied by the clamor of shouting upperclassmen. We would return to the barracks for evening accountability followed by an hour of "company administration time," which meant an hour for the cadre to make our lives miserable with inspections, errands, and any random assignment that occurred to them.

We had an hour to visit with other freshmen in our barracks before the Evening Study Period (ESP) started at 1930. ESP continued until 2230, with freshmen expected to be at their desks studying or involved in a study group in their quarters the entire time. The cadre routinely surprised us by barging into our rooms to make sure we weren't sleeping or goofing around. We had to remain dressed in a "complete uniform" at all times, and we would be "pulled" (punished) if they caught us lying down before lights-out. At 2230 steel sounded, giving us half an hour for mail call, final blister checks, and showers. We could pick up our mail at the back sally port before showering quickly, blister checks, and preparing for bed.

At 2300 taps sounded, a blessed release from the endless day. By 2400 our lights had to be out. We were only too glad to crawl into our racks by then for the precious five and a half hours of sleep allowed before the whole routine started all over again, before sunrise the next morning.

Nearly every hour of the day, we had to fall in for some kind of formation. During those first few weeks, it seemed as if I spent my life in formations. From the moment we lined up in front of the company letters on the quad at sunup, to the final blister check at night, we were continually assembled, drilled, and racked. Formation was exhausting, for we were never allowed to just stand there for long. Our cadre made us march endlessly in place, our knees drawn up to our chests at every step.

Making it worse, the whole time we were marching we had to worry about a sneak attack from one of the upperclassmen. That first month we were required to carry our *Guidons* to every formation, and the cadre would try to snatch our handbooks from us every chance they got. After jerking the books away, they would rack us for letting them do it. It was classic Citadel lose-lose intimidation. Formation required not only physical and mental endurance, but constant watchfulness. Like soldiers on the front line, we could not let down our guard for a minute—which was, of course, the point of the whole exercise.

In the case of Band Company, if we were doing drill outside on the parade ground, formation also meant marching off with our instruments to practice long before, and long after, the other companies had disbanded.

In spite of the fact that The Citadel Parades were the most high-profile events on campus, Band Company itself got constant heckling from other cadets. The lyre insignia we wore on our collars resembled the capital letter "Q," a fact that led to our being nicknamed "Q Company— Queer Company." Other cadets claimed that "Q Company" had it easier because we carried instruments instead of rifles when we marched, and because we spent so many hours practicing our music. It was a total lie. Music practice didn't make our lives easier; it made it harder. We spent just as many hours as any other company practicing our marching, but when the marching was over, we still had hours to practice with our instruments. We were usually the first company to formation in the morning, and the last one at night.

Other companies were constantly making fun of us. If a trumpet player hit a sour note, if a Band Company member made a stupid mistake, or if another company was just in a bad mood and looking for someone to laugh at, we would hear catcalls of "Q" echoing through the Corps. Obviously, my presence in the company didn't help. The other cadets took full advantage of the fact that "Q Company" had a female. It was just one more golden opportunity to embarrass us.

Of all the miseries of the constant formations, however, Sweep Details were the worst. When most people think of a line of people lifting their knees and swinging brooms in rhythm, they think of the chimney sweeps in Mary Poppins. When a Citadel knob thinks of brooms, it's a very different story. Every morning started with freshman Sweep Detail, and believe me, it was nothing like a Disney musical.

The idea was to sweep every last speck of dust from the battalion, but like everything else knob year, it was much more complicated than it sounded. The first thing we had to do after throwing our uniforms on in the morning was to meet in the squad room with our brooms to make sure all the knobs were there. Usually, we met in Reich and Brooks's room, a few doors down to my left. Once everyone was accounted for, we'd go to Mr. Dye's room together, following one another in a line, to report for duty. Whoever happened to be first that day would take two steps forward from the line in front of his door, rap sharply, and return to the line. The squad would then simultaneously pop off, "Sir, Mr. Dye, sir, members of the class of 2000 reporting as ordered, sir!" Mr. Dye would come out onto the ground-floor gallery where we stood, look us over, rack one or two of us, and then order us to begin. Like a well-organized janitorial service, we'd leap into action as the sun was coming up.

The knobs in 2nd Battalion, divided among five companies, were responsible for sweeping every speck of dirt from the quadrangle and gallery. That meant not only removing the layer of dust covering the grounds; it also meant carefully running the bristles between the crevices of the red and white squares, and along the edges of the gallery walls, where lines ran through the whitewashed cement. Band Company's assignment was to sweep each nook and cranny of the first-floor gallery until it was immaculate. Considering how long the gallery was, just cleaning it to cadre standards was hard enough. Unfortunately for me, Band Company was notorious for the fanatical requirements of its Sweep Details. By the end of first semester, most of the bristles had worn off our brooms.

But the hardest part of Sweep Detail wasn't the cleaning; it was the continual harassment. As we swept, concentrating on every speck of dust, our officers patrolled nonstop. Since we weren't allowed to look at them, it was difficult to know when one of them might suddenly appear out of nowhere. Creeping up behind us, they would grab our brooms and try to jerk them out of our hands. If they succeeded, we would be racked unmercifully for being wimps who couldn't even hold a broom. If we managed to hold on, we would still be racked, though not as severely. With someone screaming in our faces all day long, we were determined to hold on to those broomsticks. Afterward, we lined up in a row, holding our brooms stiffly out in front of us, hoping to be dismissed to quarters so we could return our brooms and prepare for breakfast mess.

Naturally the constant racking woke up everyone in the barracks, not just the knobs. Mr. Sharp's racking was so loud and obnoxious that every now and then, even the upperclassmen complained. One early morning, before the sun was even up, a furious upperclassman from Hotel Company came stalking down from the upper gallery to complain. He stomped outside in his underwear and began shouting at Mr. Sharp to "shut the hell up."

Trying to concentrate on my sweeping, I had to stifle a grin at the sight of the Hotel sergeant standing there in his "tightie whites," red-faced and screaming in rage.

Sometimes all went smoothly, but if the OC (Officer in Charge) was dissatisfied with our work, we would be punished by marking time. On command, we had to march in place, backs braced, knees high, brooms held stiffly in front of us, parallel to the ground. As we marked time, our arms beginning to ache from holding the brooms so high, our CO would pace up and down the line, racking and correcting us, one after another. Our backs weren't rigid enough, our eyes weren't straight ahead, our feet were moving too slowly or too fast, our knees weren't lifted high enough. High enough meant that our knees touched the broom handle each time we lifted them, all the way to waist level. It was difficult and exhausting, but we had to keep going until the muscles in our thighs and abs burned with pain.

If we were lucky, the sun would be up by then.

We were rarely lucky.

★ CHAPTER 8 ★

PARADE REST

One of the biggest schedule changes Hurricane Fran had caused was the postponement of the first Parade. Parade has always been at the center of Citadel life, at least in the eyes of the community. Since the days before the Civil War, when cadets marched through the streets of Charleston in a show of force, The Citadel Parade has been the high point of every week. Each Friday afternoon, the entire Corps dresses up in its shiniest brass and drills in dress uniform for admiring crowds of family, friends, and local residents. At the heart of Friday Parades is Band Company, and I was very excited about marching publicly for the first time, passing in review before my father.

Everything considered, it was lucky that Fran came along when she did, for she gave us an extra week to practice. Early and late we marched, played, and drilled, anxious to avoid embarrassing ourselves in front of the crowd. I stayed up well past taps on Thursday night, polishing my leather and brass and making certain my uniform was crisp and perfect. I examined each piece as carefully as I had measured my socks when I was five. I knew everyone would be looking at me, and I had to be perfect. I went to sleep excited, knowing my parents would be in the stands to watch me.

Parade meant visitors on campus, so I was not surprised that Sweep Detail was worse than usual the next morning. What I wasn't expecting, however, was a new cleaning duty called "Douche Detail." Named by cadets, it was renamed "Hydro Detail" my second semester (to eliminate the sexist term), Douche Detail was a wet, grueling variation of Sweep Detail. Starting with the first Parade, we had to "douche" out the barracks on Fridays.

"Douching" the battalion meant swamping out the galleries with water and brooms. That first Friday afternoon we were called to formation and then given our instructions. A group of us was ordered to go into the men's bathrooms, fill the large trash cans with water, and haul the heavy metal cans back outside onto the gallery. Once there, we were told to dump the water onto the gallery floor and begin scrubbing and sweeping with our brooms until the ground was shiny clean and damp. Each time we threw the can of water onto the walls and floor, we had to yell "Fire in the hole!" Getting the floor clean meant many trips to the bathroom to refill the trash cans, until the water rushing across the gallery floors ran clear. On one of my trips into the men's room to refill a trashcan, the platoon sergeant made me pop off as loud as I could, just because he thought it was hilarious to hear a female voice shouting in the men's bathroom. It took all of us, working at top speed, to finish the detail in time. We divided the platoon into groups of three or four and worked in shifts, alternately sweeping and dragging the heavy cans, practicing the first rule of freshman survival: Work as a team. After a while, we got the hang of it and were able to establish a rhythm that kept everyone moving.

By the time we finished, we were soaking wet and winded. Not much time was left to clean up and change into our dress uniforms in time for Parade warm-up. Getting dressed in our uniforms sounds simple to an outsider. Believe me, it was one of the hardest things I had to learn as a cadet.

I was shaking with excitement as I got dressed for my first Parade. It would be my first time in dress uniform. The uniform I was putting on was famous in South Carolina. The white shirt and light gray wool trousers represented a 150-year tradition, and being one of the first women to wear my father's uniform meant everything to me. Because Citadel cadets wear their uniforms at all times, even off campus, cadets are constantly reminded that everything they do represents the Corps. They are expected to look perfect, head to toe, at all times. I understood what was expected of me, and I was determined to be the best of the best—"hard core." My father had spent many hours that summer teaching me how to achieve the perfect shine on my shoes and brass. I'd spent dozens of hours getting my uniform in perfect condition.

Looking perfect from head to toe was complicated. It began with the haircut, which guaranteed that we looked neat and uniform. The only thing that distinguished me from the rest of Band Company was a tiny fringe of dark hair under the edge of my cover. The guys had to be clean-shaven, and we were all required to be well-scrubbed, with our teeth brushed and our ears swabbed out, before leaving quarters. If we weren't, we didn't pass inspection. The face looking back at me in the small mirror was as scrubbed as a male's, for I wasn't allowed to wear makeup—or, of course, any jewelry. For Parade, I was wearing my white garrison cap, part of the Summer Leave uniform. Getting it to stay straight was a special challenge for me, as my hat was too big. I wasn't sure if the Cadet Store didn't carry hats small enough to fit me properly, or if I had simply been given the wrong cover during the chaos of the Haze Maze.

Next I put on my shirt. Like the male cadets, I wore a bleached white T-shirt under my uniform shirt, pulled up to my neckline, smooth and wrinkle-free. The only difference was that I wore a white sports bra under the T-shirt. The white uniform shirt was the hardest part to get right. I had already heavily starched and ironed it carefully and attached the required insignias. My small brass lyre (signifying Band Company) had been polished, and positioned underneath the left breast pocket flap for company pride. I'd embarrassed myself the first day by pinning the lyre on upside down, having no idea how it was supposed to look, and had gotten severely racked for my ignorance. We wore our lyre on our collars with duty uniforms, but for Parade, we were not allowed to pin it on the collar of our Summer Leave uniform. As a matter of pride in our company, we wore it hidden under the pocket flap. I used the left-over portions of my belt as backing for the lyre. (I'd had to cut off several inches, as even the small size wrapped around my waist one and a half times.) My ID card was aligned vertically in my left pocket. Once I put the shirt on, I had to adjust it so that exactly four buttons showed above the belt, which meant that my shirt tuck had to be done just right.

Unfortunately, I inevitably ended up with three buttons showing, for my shirts were all too big for me.

By far the hardest part of dressing properly was the shirt tuck. My uniform shirt had to fit tight and smooth, lying flat under my trousers, and remain there throughout the Parade. To keep my shirt from moving, I had to wear shirt stays. Cadet shirt stays are pieces of elastic with metal clamps on the end, a lot like the garters men wear with tuxedos to keep dress socks in place. The back stays were the easiest to attach. I clipped each one to one side of my shirttail, ran it straight down the back of my leg, and attached it to my sock behind my calf. The front stays were much harder to position. I had to attach the two front stays one at a time, like a garter string. I clipped one to my right shirt hem in front. Then I wrapped the elastic around the outside of my right thigh, back under my knee, and around to the front of my calf, where I attached it to the front of my sock with the other metal clip. Afterward, I repeated the whole process with the other front stay, attaching this one to the left side of my shirtfront. The shirt was finally in place, but there was a catch. I couldn't put on my trousers and keep my shirt in place at the same time.

The only way to solve the problem was to have another cadet give you a "shirt tuck." Shirt tucks were tricky. The shirt had to be folded back tight at the side seams and held in place by one person while the other pulled up the trousers, smoothed the shirttails, and fastened the trouser buttons that held the shirt tightly against the body. I couldn't do it without my roommate. That Friday afternoon Kim held my shirt in place while I pulled up my trousers. Then I did the same for her. It was especially hard for me to get a good shirt tuck because I was so skinny that the smallest uniform shirt bagged on me. I'd tried everything from pins to tape to keep my shirt pulled tightly at the sides, and I was still worried it would come loose during Parade.

The gray trousers I wore were also carefully ironed. Once I'd pulled them on, I checked to make sure the black stripe on the side ran straight from my thigh to the side of my calf. We were required to keep our pockets empty except for one handkerchief, heavily starched, then ironed and folded, which I had to smooth flat in my right back pocket, with the flap buttoned over the top. My belt was next, which I'd treated with the same "Heel and Sole" compound we used on our shoes. My buckle, along with the rest of my brass, had been doused with lighter fluid and then shined with Brasso. I'd cleaned the inside of my buckle with a cotton swab dipped in Cutex, to remove the green grunge caused by the South Carolina humidity. Once I'd buckled my belt, I had to make a "gigline": my trousers' front zipper had to be aligned with my belt buckle and my shirt buttons to form a perfect vertical line.

Next came my shoes and socks. I wore black dress socks exactly like the men's. My shoes had required the most work to get ready. I had polished and buffed the tops until they shone like patent leather and I could literally see my reflection in them. Then I'd had to rub the heels and soles with "Heel and Sole," a heavy black rubbery compound that kept the shoes black and waterproof. Afterward, I treated the heels and soles with "Old Corps," a powerful compound that burned my fingers and nostrils but gave the shoes a deep glow.

The last three things I put on were the white webbing, shoulder boards, and black leather pouch I needed for Parade. I put one piece of webbing over my right shoulder and fastened it to the leather pouch, which rested on my left hip. The black leather pouch held any extra music, rubber bands, and other items needed by members of Band Company when we performed. Attached to the webbing, centered over my chest, was a brass plate. I had shined it until any inspecting cadet could see his reflection in it. The second piece of webbing went around my waist, then was also attached to the black pouch on my hip. Then I put on both blue shoulder boards, the right one holding the webbing in place. My knob shoulder boards held no rank as I was a member of the fourth class. It was then that I picked up my clarinet, also carefully shined for the occasion. I was ready.

I took one final look in the mirror. No amount of shirt tucking would make my shirt fit properly, but my leather and brass were the best in the company. My father wouldn't be ashamed of me.

At exactly 1500 I fell in with my company on the side of Second Battalion, ready for the Band warm-up. I took my place in line, squinting into the sun that hung low over the river, as Major Jones and Major Day spoke earnestly with the pipers who would lead us onto the field. A dozen pipers in blue tartan kilts traditionally lead the Corps onto the Parade Field, bagpipes wailing. My mind flitted briefly back to Hell Night and the wailing of the harmonica over the loudspeaker. I wondered if one of the cadets in front of me had played the background music for Mr. Butler that night. Several yards ahead of me, I could see Major Day's tall handsome figure and white hair as he pointed to something on the field. I fingered my clarinet nervously, going over the music in my mind as I waited for warm-up to begin. I wasn't sure what worried me more, missing a note or missing a step. I was scared to death I would embarrass myself. Over and over, I reminded myself not to lock my knees at attention. Our commander had warned us that if we did, we might fall over during Parade. That would be humiliating.

At 1545 I filed onto the southwest corner of Summerall Field with the rest of the Regimental Band. In less than a minute, we would lead the entire Corps of Cadets onto Summerall Field, with the pipers playing in a dazzling show of military splendor. Across from me diagonally, I could see the review stands crowded with onlookers, many of them craning their necks to get a glimpse of a loved one. Somewhere up there were my parents and my brother James. My heart beat fast, and I struggled to keep from smiling. I was so excited that I could hardly stand still. In a few moments I would march forward, the first female in the history of the Corps to step onto the Parade Field as a cadet. Tears stung my eyes. I could see media cameras flash in the distance, but I didn't care. I wondered if my parents had spotted me yet.

Sensing that the show was about to begin, the crowd began to quiet down. I kept my eyes fixed straight ahead as General Poole took his place. The hot Carolina air hung heavily over the grass, and I could see several women fanning themselves in the bleachers. Sweat trickled down the small of my back, and the shirt stay wrapped around my thigh began to itch. I didn't move. Suddenly, at a cue from the commander, the bagpipes swelled with sound, and the pipers strode onto the field, kilts swirling. A moment later, I marched with my company onto the grass behind them, clarinet held vertically in my right arm, and began the progress toward the corner of the field. It was one of the most amazing moments of my life.

I don't remember too much else about the Parade that day. I do know that none of us disgraced ourselves by falling over, dropping a rifle or an instrument, or bumping into someone. All that remains in my memory is a blur of faces, the sound of music, the aching in my neck from the long minutes at attention, and of course, the thunder of the cannons. The cannons are fired thirteen times during Citadel Parades, each explosion making the air tremble and the eardrums shiver as the acrid smell of gunpowder fills the air. I did not flinch that day, or any day after. It is a matter of pride to tolerate the earsplitting explosion without moving. When we marched off the field and turned down the lane toward our barracks forty-five minutes later, I caught a glimpse of a familiar face out of the corner of my eye. It was my mother. She had left the stands and rushed to the sidelines in hopes of getting a good look at me as I marched by. I did not turn my head, and she made no attempt to speak to me, for she knew it was against the rules. She just wanted to see for herself that her "girl" was all right. The wordless message made my heart swell.

As we passed through the sally port after that first Parade, I felt a rush of pride and gratitude. I was so proud to be a member of Band Company. Even with all the stress of the last three weeks, there had been moments that were almost magical. Lined up on the Parade Field in the hours before dawn, I had watched the mist float upward as the sun crested the horizon and the sound of bagpipes swirled around me. Striding onto the field that afternoon, behind those same pipers, I felt a rare joy coursing through my veins. For the first time in my life, I was a part of something wonderful and unique.

When evening darkened, I leaned on my windowsill and gazed at the empty Parade Field as my classmates' trumpets played taps. The lights in the battalions disappeared one by one, like candles being snuffed out.

That night they played echo taps, the most haunting music of all. Echo taps were played to honor the passing of Citadel graduates, and the sounds echoing through the silent campus that night were a poignant reminder of my own mortality, and of the generations of cadets who had gazed out this same window. Two trumpet players, standing side by side in front of the battalion microphone, played the farewell, the second instrument echoing the sound of the first. It brought me to tears, both for the sorrow and for the beauty of the notes that reverberated through me. The silence that followed, after the incessant racket of the day, felt like a benediction, and I prayed as I gazed out into the darkness.

As I lay in my rack that Friday night, I was filled with pride to be another link in the century-and-a-half long gray line, proud especially to be a member of Band Company, whose honor it was to honor The Citadel. I would not have transferred to another company, or another college, for the world.

Aerial photograph of The Citadel campus during Friday afternoon parade

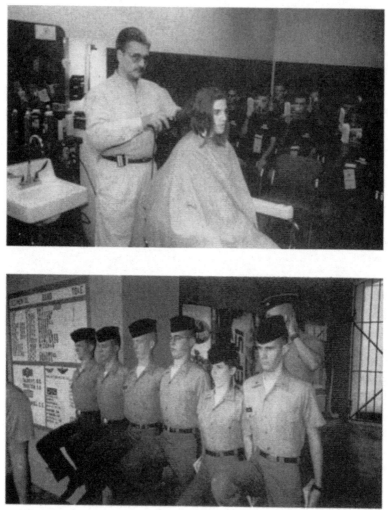

TOP: The first haircut of a female knob by Citadel barber, Dave Creaturo

ABOVE: First platoon marking time at formation in the back sally port of 2nd battalion. Front (*left to right*) Tim Brock, Mark Howell, Bryan King, Ryan Jones, Nancy Mace, and Evan Reich); Back, Jay Kaufman.

ABOVE: Cadet Corporal Kris Mitchell teaching Nancy during N-knob Salute Education. Cadre (*left to right*) Kris Mitchell and William Simpson; Knobs (*left to right*) Dave Maher, Nancy Mace, Mark Howell, and Bryan King.

LEFT: OD (Officer of the Day) Cadet Danny Cooper posing with Cadet Private Mace, spring 1997

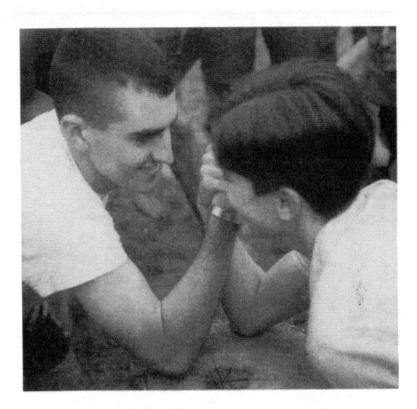

OPPOSITE, ABOVE: Hell week in 2nd battalion quadrangle. Cadre (*left to right*) Kris Mitchell, Ben Ingram, Rob Hood, and Chip Shuler; Knobs (*right to left*) Bryan King, Mark Howell, Nancy Mace, Dave Maher, Alex Spara, Cadet Robinson, and William Carroll.

OPPOSITE, BELOW: Hell week on the Summerall Parade Field. Cadre, Jason Cain; Knobs (*left to right*) Delmer Powell, Matthew Erkinger, Nancy Mace, and Dave Maher.

ABOVE: Scott Wizeman and Nancy arm wrestling during the "Calling out" ceremony at the Knob Company Party

ABOVE: The Citadel Cadet Honor Guard with former United States President George Bush at Charleston's Omni Hotel

OPPOSITE, TOP LEFT: Petra and Nancy during Parents' Weekend, 1997

OPPOSITE, TOP RIGHT: Petra and Nancy dressed for Homecoming Weekend, 1998

OPPOSITE, BOTTOM: Petra and Nancy during a May 1997 press conference at the Alumni House in Charleston, South Carolina

ABOVE: Walking through the
ring with her father during the
"Ring Hop"

RIGHT: Nancy and her father
showing off their rings—the old
and the new on "Ring Day," in
front of Summerall Chapel

ABOVE: A young Cadet James E. Mace receiving his class of 1963 Citadel diploma from President General Mark Clark

LEFT: Nancy receiving her diploma on Graduation Day, May 8, 1999, from her father, Commandant of Cadets, Brigadier General James E. Mace, '63

ABOVE: The Mace family, Change of Command, June 1987. Back *(left to right)* General Mace, Mary, Beth Anne, and Anne Mace; Front, James and Nancy.

LEFT: About to begin a one-mile race, Nancy, age seven, and her father, Fort Benning, Georgia

OPPOSITE, ABOVE: James, age two, Nancy, age four, Panama, 1981

OPPOSITE, BELOW: Nancy and James, spring 1998

ABOVE: Walking under the sword detail (a military wedding tradition) with Lieutenant Christopher P. Niemiec on their wedding day, April 29, 2000.

OPPOSITE: Graduation Day standing outside parents' campus home, front of quarters 2, The Citadel.

★ CHAPTER 9 ★

GOING THE DISTANCE

On the first morning of October, I smiled as I turned the page in my organizer. I had survived Hell Week, Hurricane Fran, and a month few grown men could get through. "Not bad for a girl," I told myself as I dressed for formation. I had already forgotten the knob's first rule: Never let your guard down.

The day began well. I attended an AUSA reception that evening along with two of my classmates and a handful of other cadets from Band, which meant a trip off campus in salt and pepper (full dress uniform) and a real meal, free from the horrors of the Mess Hall. We would be posting the colors for the Army event. As we left campus in the car that evening, the upperclassmen who rode with us started nicknaming us knobs. Corney was "Snake Eye," Chinn was "Grunt," and I was "Lady J." I loved being dressed in my dress uniform, and my heart swelled with pride as I helped post the AUSA flag. I met several generals, ate a wonderful meal, and received a commemorative coin with my fellow cadets for the good work we did. It was the first of many times I would represent my class, the first of many times I would know I had represented them well. It felt good, good enough that I didn't even mind when an officer referred to me as "sir." I was getting used to that.

I returned to campus after nine to find a care package from my mother waiting in the mailroom, which lifted my spirits even more. I had begun to wonder if I was ever going to get a box of "necessities" from home, and I had been complaining to my mom by e-mail for weeks, pointing out that Kim and all the other girls—and guys—had received care packages by now. Mail had become a sensitive issue with me, for though I got more mail than anyone else in Band Company, most of it was from strangers.

From my first mail call during Hell Week, I found my mailbox stuffed with letters and messages from people I had never met, almost all of it supporting my efforts to survive at The Citadel. I was surprised and touched by the large amount of support mail, which I rarely had time to answer, but it also created problems for me. The other cadets saw me returning to my room every night after formation with stacks of letters, while many of them received no mail at all. It created resentment and led to extra racking from some of the upperclassmen. At the same time I was buried in letters from strangers, I received almost no mail from home. I wrote Mom and Dad and James almost daily, letting off steam and sharing my small victories, yet very little came back, and it bothered me. I knew how much my parents loved me; their presence at chapel and Parades was an ongoing example of their unconditional support. "Still, a letter every few days wouldn't have killed them," I thought as I walked back to my quarters.

That night, as I carried my care package back to my room, I chatted happily with my classmates and even shared a few of the "goodies" from the box they eagerly prodded me to open. Back in my quarters, I munched contentedly on granola bars and fruit jellies (my favorite) as I sorted through the rest of my mail and then flipped on my computer to check my e-mail and send a thank-you to my mom. I was used to e-mail from strangers by then, so I continued to chew as I read yet another "letter" from an unknown sender.

Suddenly I felt the granola stick in my throat as I read the salutation: "Bitch." Coughing and swallowing gulps of water, my eyes ran involuntarily over the phrases that followed: "ugly bitch," "ruined the school," "everyone hates you," "slut," "disgrace." Anger welled up, and with it, all the old pain. I was getting used to the racking and catcalls on campus, but the filthy words, seeping into my private quarters through the monitor on my desk, made me feel violated. It was as though the faceless writer was there with me, having crept into my room while I was gone. I looked for the source heading, but there wasn't one. I tried to return the message, typing "return to sender" in the subject line and hitting "reply," but it kept coming back. After several tries, I gave up and deleted it. "Loser," I said to myself, "stupid jerk! Got nothing better to do than write nasty letters to a stranger?" Still, it was hard to get it out of my mind. I tried to study before lights-out, but I couldn't get rid of the prickle between my shoulder blades or the heat that stung my cheeks. Why had he said those things? What made people think they had the right to do that to me?

I knew that if I dwelled on those things, I would go crazy, so I did my best to shut the letter out of my mind. Meanwhile, life in the battalion went on, and it was all I could do to keep up with it. I was surprised to find how quickly I had adjusted to the basics of knob existence. Most of the rules controlling my daily life had already become second nature. At lunch and dinner mess, we occasionally took turns reciting the list:

• Knobs will instantly obey the order of any upperclass cadet without question.

• Knobs will salute all officers.

• Knobs will offer no excuse for misconduct unless asked to explain their actions.

• When reporting to an upperclass cadet's room, knobs will remove their cap, knock twice, and report in a military manner.

• Knobs are prohibited from grassy areas, except during PT, formation, or Parades; and from the quadrangle, except during formation.

• Knobs are prohibited from all streets on the campus, except when crossing at an intersection, and must proceed in a line on the right side of sidewalks only.

• Knobs are prohibited from walking on the Avenue of Remembrance sidewalk and must walk only in the gutter.

• Knobs are prohibited from occupying certain buildings at all times, and from using the main entrances of most buildings. They are to use the side entrances only.

• Knobs must be braced at all times outside their quarters, run everywhere within battalions, and are to proceed only at double time along sidewalks.

• Knobs will ask permission to "drive by" before passing upper-class cadets on galleries or stairs, and will halt and stand at attention whenever an upperclass cadet passes them.

• Knobs will not smoke out of doors in uniform.

• Knobs will never appear outside their rooms except in proper uniform, clean and polished.

• During study periods in their rooms, knobs must wear a proper uniform, such as pajamas and robe, at all times.

• Knobs will read all company bulletin boards twice daily and be responsible for their content.

• Knobs will attend all Citadel football games.

The last rule, requiring us to attend all football games, should have been the easiest one on the list. It should, in fact, have been fun. Who doesn't like to go to football games and cheer for their team? I'd always loved sports. I soon learned that for me, though, it was the hardest rule to keep. As a member of Band Company, I played and marched at all home games. The performances always drew attention to me, since I was out on the field with the Regimental Band. Football games drew large numbers of alumni, family, and friends of cadets, and it was here that I first experienced genuine cruelty at The Citadel.

Almost from the beginning, football games were a nightmare for me. As the band marched from the barracks to the stadium, we would pass hundreds of spectators, many of them wives, mothers, and girl-friends of the cadets. Some of the women walked next to me as I marched at the far end of my platoon in formation, taunting me as I walked. Some made fun of me for being ugly or butch, with my hair cut off and my boys' clothes. Others called me a slut or a whore who was really at The Citadel to "do it" with every guy in the Corps. Some called me a "dyke" who couldn't make it as a woman. Many simply shouted, "We hate you, bitch!" or "You ruined our school!" There was nothing I could do but keep on marching, eyes straight ahead, their words echoing through my head as my stomach filled with acid and my eyes burned.

Walking to the restroom during games was another ordeal. Some spectators made nasty remarks as I passed the stands. When I went into the ladies' room, the women often would stare and make sarcastic remarks or tell me to go to the men's room. Walking back to my company, more shouts of "Bitch!" or "Dyke!" would follow me.

Ironically, the worst abuse in public usually came from other females. I was astonished at what came out of the mouths of these perfectly groomed women. So much for the famed gentility of the Southern Belle. I soon learned why the wealthy Charleston women who formed the backbone of Citadel social support were sometimes referred to as the "SOBs." The letters literally meant "South of Broads," referring to Broad Street, the avenue that traditionally divided the wealthy section of Charleston from the poor. I, however, understood all too well why those particular letters had been chosen to describe them. I knew who the real bitches were.

More than anyone, though, I came to dread one particular alumnus. He came to every game, always roaring drunk, and he seemed obsessed with me. The minute Band marched out onto the field, he would be down out of the stands, drunk and abusive. A real exhibitionist, he was always doing things to draw attention to himself, and usually to me. His favorite pep song was "Hawaii Five-O," and he always came down to the field when we played it. One time he even had some guys carry him down on a surfboard. I came to dread that song.

During halftime, he would come looking for me in the bleachers where I sat with my fellow cadets. I could feel my body go rigid the minute I caught sight of him. Weaving his way down the row to me, he would intentionally step on my feet, wiping his muddy soles on my carefully polished leather shoes until they were smeared and dirty. Then he would laugh and point at my feet, telling me that I was a disgrace to the uniform. Afterward, he would lean into my face, his breath stinking of alcohol, and whisper a steady stream of obscenities into my ear. I was the little slut who was "fucking my way through the ranks" and "ruining his school." I would sit at attention while he whispered, staring straight ahead, my cheeks burning, my eyes smarting with tears, as nausea rose and nearly overpowered me. His breath was hot on my neck, and when he poked me, I always wondered where his fingers would land next. It took every ounce of strength to keep the tears back, not to run, for it was the high school football players all over again, pressing me against the wall. Struggling not to vomit, I would whisper words in my head as I waited for him to give up and go away: "Asshole, fucker, bastard, idiot." The obscenities became a sort of mental chant that helped me endure the anger, the revulsion, and the fear.

The worst part was that no one helped me. The other cadets in my company just sat there, pretending they didn't see a thing. Some of them looked upset, but didn't seem to know what to do. "Still," I wondered, "why don't my platoon officers interfere? Don't they see what is going on?" Once or twice Mr. Dye came to my aid and politely escorted the alumnus away. The relief I felt at those moments was short-lived, for I knew the old SOB would be back the next week, and the one after that. I couldn't understand why he hated me so much. What had I ever done to him?

Soon health problems began to add to my misery. As October wore on and the weather cooled off, I developed a nagging cold and a constant ache in my neck and pelvis. There were mornings when I could hardly drag myself from my bunk to face the day. By the second Friday of the month, I had pelvic pain too severe to ignore and was sent to the infirmary, where I was told I had pulled my hamstring and strained either my groin or my hip flexor. I was also X-rayed for stress fractures in my pelvis and excused from physical training until the results came back. Even as the doctor filled out the paperwork, I groaned inwardly. An excuse from physical training (XPT) meant guaranteed racking. XPTs were always looked at suspiciously by other cadets (XPT equaled "loafer"), and as a female, I would be even more suspect. Aside from the usual stigma of "female problems," people still made jokes about Shannon Faulkner checking into the infirmary shortly after arriving at The Citadel because she "couldn't take it." Worse yet, both Kim and Jeanie had repeatedly been XPTed for suspected stress fractures and other complaints. They hadn't been drilling since the third week of school. Now another female was taken out of physical training for a while. I was willing to suffer almost any amount of misery before dropping out of physical training completely.

I kept the XPT to myself until after Parade that day. Instead, I returned to my company from the infirmary for the usual Friday

"Douche Detail." That afternoon as we swamped out the barracks, the upperclass decided to turn out in full force to "help" the knobs with the detail—lucky us. After the usual screaming and harassment that went with Douche Details, Mr. Schuler (our platoon sergeant) snatched my hat off as I toed the line in the quad, bracing with my fellow knobs. Tossing my hat into a trash can filled with dirty water, he swished it around until it was soaked, then crammed it back onto my head. Not daring to wipe away the dirty water now streaming into my eyes, I stood at attention as Mr. Schuler repeated the process with every other knob in my platoon. We were then ordered to complete the detail, and when we finished, ordered to toe the line and brace one more time.

Unfortunately, we weren't done yet. Mr. Schuler chose that day to assign us a new form of clean-up: Dip Spit Detail.

Few things are more disgusting than dip spit. Dip was more popular in the battalion than cigarettes, and it sometimes seemed like half the Corps had a mouthful of Copenhagen or Red Man. They would scoop a fingerful of the shredded tobacco out of the cans with their fingers and wedge it between their front teeth and their lower lip. It made their chins protrude like baboons. Sitting and studying in their rooms, cadets would soak up the nicotine and lean over to spit the dark brown, smelly tobacco juice into whatever was handy. Some used paper cups or Coke cans; others spit directly into the metal trash cans. Kim took up the habit shortly after school started, and I would come back to the room to find our trash full of tobacco clumps and dark brown saliva. On warm days cadets would sit outside and chew, and if they forgot to bring a cup with them, they'd just spit the tobacco juice onto the ground. It was disgusting.

Wads of tobacco and brown saliva would mix with the mold growing there in the Charleston heat and humidity, producing dark stains on the whitewash. When the spit stains became noticeable to the upperclassmen, we had to clean it up. That afternoon Mr. Schuler pointed out the spittle on the walls and floors of the gallery, then ordered us to haul out cloths, brushes, and hot soapy water. As soon as we did, we had to get down on our knees and scrub the crevices with toothbrushes, and the walls and galleries with hand brushes, until every speck of brown came loose. It was the grossest thing I'd ever done, and kneeling on the stone flags to scour off the tobacco stains made the pain in my pelvis even worse. By the time we were finally released to put away our tools and dress for Parade, I could feel myself shaking. Pain ran over me in waves. Tears filled my eyes as I returned to my room to change, and I fought to keep anyone from seeing them. Showing weakness was just asking for trouble. It wasn't safe.

I missed one or two PT sessions, until my X rays came back and showed I had strained, not fractured, my pelvis. I convinced the doctor to let me return to normal training, promising to report back if I got worse. I still hurt, but with physical therapy the pain was manageable, whereas dropping out of training would mean pain of a different kind. I had to keep up with my platoon.

Apart from the physical wear and tear of physical and military training, we knobs were constantly run ragged by the cadets who outranked us. One of our most exhausting chores was laundry run. Every Wednesday, right after classes ended, Band Company's clean laundry would be dropped off by laundry services at the back sally port of Barracks 2. Eighteen inch by 6" brown paper bundles would be stacked several feet high, ready for delivery to upperclassmen. The knobs were the deliverymen. As soon as the bundles arrived, we would gather in one of the squad rooms to take a head count and organize. We always made sure the whole team was there and ready to go. Then we'd divvy up the assignments and get to work on the bundles.

The size of the bundles was no problem. Even a "girl" like me could lift them easily. It was the constant running that made Laundry Detail so exhausting. Packages had to be delivered one at a time, and knobs were required to circle the perimeter of the quad, always at a run, to make each delivery. If we ran across a cadet officer from another company on the way, we had to stop and ask permission to drive by, which meant guaranteed racking. Afterward, when we arrived at the upperclassman's door, we had to knock, announce ourselves, wait for the order to enter, then carry the bundle inside. Once inside, if the cadet was waiting for his laundry, he would usually rack us also—or worse.

Being told to drop and do push-ups was always a possibility, for though the practice was against the rules, it was sometimes done behind closed doors. Usually, though, the favorite method of harassment during Laundry Details was to be ordered into the cadet's clothing press. I would be ordered to step on the bottom edge of the full-press, balanced on my toes and tensing every muscle in an effort not to fall backward. Then I had to brace while facing the back of the tall metal compartment, still holding the bundle of clean laundry in my arms. It was incredibly difficult and uncomfortable, and all my muscles cried out in protest.

If I was lucky, I would be ordered to set down the laundry and remove myself after a minute or two. If the cadet was in a bad mood, however, I would be told I had delivered the laundry all wrong and to do it again. That meant shouting, "Sir, yes, sir!", then leaving his quarters to run all the way around the quad and return to his front door, where the ritual would begin all over again. Mr. Ingram was notorious for racking the knobs on his laundry run. On bad days, he would make us run around the quad several times, being racked between each run, before he would finally accept his laundry bundle. Sometimes I felt like it would never end.

After we had delivered all the upperclassmen's laundry, we still had to get our own. By that time we were worn out, but we still had to carry the bundles back to our quarters and arrange them according to formation in our drawers. The first time I opened one of my own laundry bundles, I discovered to my horror that half my clothing had been ruined. My white sports bras were brown and yellow and covered with holes. After replacing them several times (for knobs would get racked for stained clothing), I finally learned to keep a few good pairs of underwear and bras to place in my drawers for inspection, stowing them separately from the others. I would take the good pairs home on leave to wash them there. Replacing them constantly was just too expensive.

Laundry duty was typical of what upperclassmen thought of as their "sacred obligation" to make the knobs' lives as miserable as their own cadre had once made theirs. Most of the daily harassment I endured was no different from other freshmen. Upperclass cadets loved to intimidate us; it was just part of the system. One cadet actually put tacks on the bottoms of his shoes so we would hear him coming, an ominous *click, click, click* on the gallery. Physical aggression against knobs was forbidden in the Corps, and I had little fear that anyone would harm me physically. Every now and then, though, I would encounter a truly menacing figure among the cadets. One psycho from Echo Company gave me the chills, staring at me in a dirty, threatening manner and making frightening threats under his breath. On several occasions he threatened to body slam me, but he never did. He was punished for his aggression, which eventually got him kicked out of the College. Contrary to rumors, genuine viciousness wasn't tolerated. Our chain-of-command watched out for us.

It was only when the racking got personal that it bothered me. One day, when I stumbled over a Mess Fact at lunch, I was told I had the functioning ability of a ten-year-old. I had been going to see Dr. Zaremba all that week, and I wondered if my mess carver had found out I had a learning disability. His comment might just have been a coincidence, but I felt humiliated anyway. Sometimes my mind just went blank, and the words wouldn't come out. It made me feel stupid again, just like I did when I was younger.

Sometimes, though, I knew the harassment was because I was female. One night in mid-October, holed up my room to study, I heard the sound of running feet and loud voices chanting, *"We love 98/Last class/All male"* in rhythm. A large group of cadets was doing a PT run through the barracks, sounding off as they ran. The shouting and the pounding of feet went on continuously for more than fifteen minutes, until I gave up even trying to concentrate on my books. At last it grew quiet, and a few minutes later Mr. Rawlinson, my first sergeant, knocked on my door. Entering the room, he said, "As the highest-ranking junior of our company, I apologize for my class." He went on to explain that he had not taken part in the run himself, then asked me if I understood. I told him I did. I understood all too well.

Another evening, as I returned alone to my room from studying in the library, I was stopped by two Band Company corporals. Ordering me to brace, they started to rack me, telling me that I was the worst knob in the company, the worst even of the four girl cadets. As proof that I was nothing but a shitbag, they told me that Colonel Lackey had described my appearance as the worst of any female knob. They were referring to a meeting I'd attended with the colonel the day before, with only ten minutes notice, after a particularly dirty Sweep Detail. It was totally unfair, for I had not been notified about the meeting in time to clean my uniform.

As a knob, I was not allowed to defend myself to either cadet. Instead, I had to alternately brace in silence or pop off, "Sir, no excuse, sir!" I had to bite the inside of my lip to keep tears of rage from welling up, and the effort made sweat run down my body in streams. Finally, one of them leaned in close and told me that they were going to make me "all theirs." I felt sick to my stomach. Everybody knew that knobs were sometimes "claimed" by upperclassmen for intensely abusive relationships. It wasn't supposed to happen, but sometimes it did. It was bad enough when they got ahold of a male knob. What would they do to a female?

I forced the images out. I could not afford to give in to their tactics of fear and intimidation. As the screaming continued, I could feel my entire body trembling. Anger overcame the humiliation, and for a moment I wanted to just crawl out of my body and go to my room where I could have a moment's peace. After a while, they seemed to get tired of harassing me and excused me to my room. I posted to my quarters at double time, whispering obscenities under my breath, desperate for a moment to myself.

As I neared the darkness of the front sally port, I could make out yet another upperclassman, and for one horrified moment, I thought the racking was going to start all over again. I sighed with relief when I saw that it was Mr. Wizeman. Ordering me to halt, he casually asked me if I got harassed very often when I was alone. I stumbled out a reply, not knowing whether I should tell him what had just happened. I finally settled on, "Sir, yes, sir!" He looked at me shrewdly, started to say something, then apparently thought better of it. Instead, he rapped out an order for me to return to my quarters. I hurried away.

He never said a word to me about what had happened with Mr. Kaufman and Mr. Ingram that night. Yet, I noticed that though they continued to rack me now and then, they never repeated their threat to make me "their knob."

The month seemed endless. There were days when the harassment seemed to permeate every level of the battalion, days when even we knobs were drawn into the power plays. Most Band Company officers acted professionally, but a few could be truly sadistic. When a cadet officer ordered me to call a cadet corporal named Mitchell "a girl" to humiliate him one day, I did it. So did the rest of my platoon. Afterward, I felt guilty and ashamed. I was no better than the cadets who bullied me. I learned a new phrase that day: "Sir, requesting permission to use better judgment, sir!" In the months that followed, I worked hard at knowing when to use that phrase.

Matters came to a head for me near the end of October, when ABC aired a "Turning Point" episode about me. The College administrators had urged me to do the inerview on behalf of The Citadel, and I had done it to oblige them, but with great reluctance. Being the focus of that kind of attention is the worst thing that can happen to a knob. It is asking for trouble, and I was scared to death about what might happen to me after the show aired. I'd already had several anonymous e-mail threats, and one morning I'd gotten up to find GO HOME, BITCH written in shaving cream on the door to my quarters. Worried about possible retaliation after the TV show, the administration took precautions to guarantee my safety. Guards were posted at my door on the night following the broadcast, and my cadet corporal was especially watchful to make certain I remained safe. I knew Band Company would watch out for me, but I wasn't so sure about the others. Echo and Hotel Company were both in the battalion, too, on the galleries above me, and I knew they hated me. I really wasn't sure what they were capable of.

To my infinite relief, I passed the night in peace. No one bothered me. I got some extra racking the next day, and a few catcalls, but that was nothing. I'd expected much worse. In fact, I was amazed when a few cadets actually said something positive to me. One told me I had done "pretty well," or at least that I hadn't been "as bad as they expected." Later that day, in my math class, a senior private from another company even paid me a backhanded compliment. This guy often made fun of me in class or cracked jokes at my expense, but his comments were never mean-spirited, and I knew he was just teasing me. The morning after the broadcast he announced rather loudly during math that I had "actually looked pretty cute" before I came to El Cid and turned into "an ugly little knob." In his weird way, I knew he meant it as a compliment, and I felt my face burn. I also knew that he wasn't hitting on me, just letting me know that I was okay. It was kind of nice.

Ironically, my biggest problem in the barracks that month turned out to be with another woman—my roommate, Kim. Things were increasingly tense between us. For one thing, I was always getting in trouble for things she did. We had room inspection every morning, and we knew we'd be written up if we didn't meet the standard, yet Kim was a slob, leaving her things lying all over. The third week of school we'd been written up for a "gross room" because Kim had left a mess for an MRI, and I had to sit confinements for Kim's carelessness. It wouldn't have been so bad if she had apologized to me for the mistake, but instead she just blew me off when I told her she had to keep her things squared away. After that I found myself cleaning up for both of us, just to avoid getting punished again for her mess.

Smoking was another problem. Cigarette smoke got into my contacts and hurt my eyes, and Kim had promised not to smoke in our room. She not only went back on her word almost immediately, but worse, she lied about it. When I returned to find our room filled with cigarette smoke, Kim would deny knowing anything about it. Even when I found her cigarette butts in our trash can and ashes on the floor, she would look me in the eye and tell me she had no idea how they got there. It made me furious. I hate to be lied to, and the lying started to bother me more than the smoke. I couldn't trust her.

The most serious problem between us had to do with the hours we kept. I was exhausted almost all the time, and I desperately needed to sleep at night. The pain in my groin and the continual colds made sleeping hard to begin with, but Kim's computer habits made it impossible. We had agreed at the beginning to follow the school's "lights-out" policy. She broke that agreement too, staying up all night "chatting" on the Internet, often with Jeanie there, too. She had learned that if she covered the small window above our door with a blanket, she could turn on the desk light and play all night on her computer without getting caught. Between the light and the noise in our small room, it was impossible for me to fall deeply asleep. Some mornings I would be in tears after being kept awake all night.

I suspected that Kim was heading for serious trouble when she came back some weekends smelling like alcohol. And we couldn't get away with the same things the male cadets could, as nobody said a word if a guy drank too much, but everyone held the females to a different standard. I was always being called a drunken bitch, even though I hadn't had a drink in two years. Besides, drinking heavily when you were the only girl was dangerous, and I knew that some of these guys hated us and wanted to put us in our place.

Unable to relax anywhere after a while, even in my own room, I could feel pressure building up inside me until I sometimes thought I would explode. I knew I had to find a way to cope with the stress if I was going to survive. Playing my clarinet helped, and so did PT once my groin healed. I bought a small notebook and began keeping a journal of my emotions, releasing my pent-up anger and pain on paper. At night I would write at my desk, gazing out at the Parade Field, mist shimmering in the moonlight, reminding myself why I had come here. When writing in my journal wasn't enough to relax me, I would do curls and push-ups until my muscles began to release some of their tension. Afterward, I would lie in bed, listening to my classmate's trumpet playing taps, praying silently in the darkness, praying for strength and for courage to go the distance.

CHAPTER 10

BROTHERHOOD

If it hadn't been for the support of my family, I don't think I could have endured it all. Week after week, my parents were in the stands to watch Friday Parade, and on Sunday mornings, they were in chapel. Even though I was rarely allowed to speak to them, I always knew they were there. When Parents' Weekend rolled around, Mom and Dad and James were there bright and early Saturday morning, to tour the barracks and see my room. My father pointed out the room on the second gallery where he had lived as a cadet. It was exciting to remember that I was now living in the same battalion my father had once lived in.

Later that morning there was a special parade, and my mother was waiting for me as I came off the Parade Field. As soon as we were dismissed from formation, I walked into her arms. The campus was crowded with visitors who had driven down to see their sons and daughters.

As we strolled across the grass behind the stands, my mother's arm around my shoulders, a well-dressed woman in her forties approached us. She was beautifully dressed in a long, sheer sundress, with a broad-brimmed hat to protect her from the Charleston sun and artfully applied makeup. At first I thought she was going to speak to my mother, but when I caught the expression on her face and the direction of her glance, I felt my stomach knot up. Ignoring my mother, she stepped in front of me, blocking my path, her face only a few inches from mine.

Her voice was shaking with anger as she grabbed my arm and hurled the now-familiar stream of abuse at me for being "the bitch that ruined The Citadel." I felt the usual nausea begin to rise, but as it did, my mother's hand tightened on my shoulder. Glancing to my left, I saw Mom's slender face harden, her bones coming into sharp relief and her eyes boring through the woman. I had seen my mother use that same withering stare to quiet a classroom. I slipped my arm around my mother's waist. Mom didn't say a word, but as the woman gradually became aware of her, the woman's words slowed and faltered. Finally, with one last half-hearted insult, she walked away. Arms still around each other, my mother and I walked back to the bleachers in silence.

The next morning there was a special chapel service for cadets and their families. After services, my parents took me downtown for lunch to my favorite restaurant. Dad and I took turns telling funny stories about our Citadel classmates while we ate, and I laughed so hard, I nearly spit out my food. It felt wonderful just to be with them, to see the pride and affection on Dad's face as I shared my cadet adventures. Afterward, we wandered around Charleston, through the historic marketplace with its souvenirs of the Old South, weaving between carriages that took visitors on tours of Rainbow Row with its carefully restored mansions. The occasional "souvenirs" left steaming in piles on the streets by the carriage horses only added to the fun. By the time we all piled into Dad's Cadillac for the ride back to campus, my mood was mellow. The sky faded from pink to gray as we neared the campus's white walls, already shrouded in the evening shadows. The Citadel looked beautiful at sunset, like a gleaming castle from another century. It had been a glorious day.

Parents' Day also marked the official end to the "rule" of the cadre over the freshmen, but contrary to appearances, this was not a good thing for us knobs. We were now fair game for any upperclassman on campus. The cadre had ridden us hard, but they had also protected us during these last weeks, for they were responsible for our training and welfare. Now that we had learned the basics of cadet life, the cadre wouldn't be around to protect us all the time.

Anyone who wanted to harass us would now be free to do so. Hazing was forbidden, but upperclassmen still knew endless ways to make a knob's life miserable. As I got out of the car in the lane next to my barracks, I asked my brother to stand on the corner and "watch me home." He wasn't allowed to walk me back to my room, as visiting hours were now over, but I hoped that the sight of him would discourage other cadets from stopping and racking me. I trotted toward the front sally port without getting stopped, then rounded the entrance, out of his sight. Just as I thought I was safe, I came face-to-face with the guard, who ordered me to halt and brace. I heard the car door slam and my family drive away as he started to speak.

"Mace, you go to church?"

"Sir, yes, sir."

"What denomination are you, Mace?"

"Sir, Protestant, sir."

"You pray a lot, Mace?"

"Sir, yes, sir."

"You better, Mace, because that is the only thing that might get you and your shitbag classmates through next week!"

I took a long swallow and said, "Sir, yes, sir," once more. He racked me for a few more minutes, and when he finally dismissed me, I posted back to my quarters at record pace. I just wanted to "get out of Dodge" before he got ahold of me again.

As hard as it was at times, I was discovering that my family was not my only support. Even within the Corps, there were sources of comfort and encouragement. The administration regularly invited cadets to their homes for a home-cooked meal, and midway through October, I also received a dinner invitation. Shined and pressed in our dress uniforms, I walked with three of my classmates to Colonel Rembert's house for dinner one pleasant fall evening. Colonel Rembert was a tall man with a deep Charleston accent, something of a campus legend. He had been rumored to have written articles for the *Brigadier*, the Citadel paper, under a female pen name, and though something of an eccentric by Citadel standards, he was well-liked among the cadets. The colonel and his wife treated us to home-cooked lasagna, salad, bread, cookies, and pie. We all ate until we were bursting, grateful for the chance to eat in peace in a comfortable dining room, without a single Mess Fact to recite. Afterward, we hurried back to the battalion together, so full it was hard to walk fast enough. Those were the times when I loved The

Citadel, those precious moments when being female didn't matter and I was just another knob, hanging out with my classmates after a good meal.

The weeks also brought other friendships, relationships that kept me going when times got hard. By a funny coincidence, I was assigned to a squad with the only black, and the only Jewish knobs in my platoon. Evan Reich was a Jewish boy from Charleston who played the tuba and Allyn Brooks was an African American psychology major from New Jersey who played the trumpet. Together, our three-knob squad formed the most unusual combination of knobs in the company. Politely nicknamed the "Diversity Squad," we referred to ourselves as the "Odd Squad: the Jew, the Black, and the Chick," and quickly became very tightly bonded. Each of us knew how it felt to be different, to be "the only one," and in spite of our personality differences, we developed a strong bond. We watched out for one another, encouraged one another. If I needed a place to talk or cry or vent, I could go to Reich and Brooks's room and know I would be safe. Soon I began carrying my leather and brass down to their room for nightly shine parties that were as much for moral support as for passing the next morning's inspection. It was odd, I sometimes thought. All those years in high school, I'd never felt like I fit in. Here, even with all the harassment I took for being female, there were moments when I felt like—for the first time in my life—I really belonged.

For the most part, the company knobs stuck together, out of both survival instinct and loyalty. The teamwork that our cadre had drilled into us day after day had its effect. When we finally got our first weekend leave, nearly all the Band Company knobs left campus together. Freshmen weren't allowed to have cars, so all of us walked together through the narrow streets of old Charleston, strung out along the sidewalk like a flock of gray doves. Cadets wear their uniforms at all times, even off campus, so most people turned around to look as we tramped the long miles into downtown Charleston, laughing and joking as we went. Brooks and Reich walked on either side of me. No one we passed paid me special notice, for in uniform—with my skinny, flat-chested body and buzzed hair—I looked like just another male cadet. By the time we reached Market Street, we were starved, so we crowded into a pizza parlor and crammed ourselves until we couldn't move. Afterward, some of the guys went looking for liquor, but I stayed behind with Reich and Brooks to stock up on junk food at my favorite specialty store. Armed with jelly beans and gourmet cocoa, we met up with the rest of our classmates for the return to campus. We made it back just in time for All-In.

Waving good-bye to my friends, I changed into my pajamas and crawled into bed. Lying there, staring out at the Parade Field and munching jelly beans as I waited for taps, I smiled with contentment. Sometimes it was good to just be one of the guys. I knew that I had experienced an evening most girls would never have in their lives. For a while tonight, most of my classmates had forgotten I was a female; I was just a knob like them, with an entire evening of freedom. It felt great.

Strange as it may sound, I even developed decent relationships with some of the same upperclassmen who harassed me. I turned out to have a knack for accounting, and when word got around that I was doing well in class, other cadets started coming to me for help. I was shocked when, one evening during study period, my old enemy Mr. Kaufman walked into my room with two cadets from Echo Company, both of them needing help with their accounting homework. After asking me to tutor them, he told me that he might be back himself before midnight, for help with his own homework. I was floored. Two hours earlier, he had been racking me as I toed the line. Now he was here in my room, telling me fairly politely that he needed my help with one of his classes. Amazing! Before the month was out, I found that I'd become the unofficial accounting tutor, spending many evenings helping other cadets with their homework. This didn't stop them from racking me, of course, but somehow it didn't bother me as much. We all knew they'd need my help again before the day was out.

Little by little, I was building up a network of support in the battalion that made my life bearable, if not easy. Word had gotten out that I was a good student, and soon I came to expect regular visits from upperclassmen looking for help with accounting or English. It was good for my self-esteem, and I would smile when they left, knowing that I was earning their respect, if not their approval.

Mr. Kaufman not only brought other cadets to me for help; after a while, he started coming to me himself for help with English. We were both in the same English class. The results were sometimes funny. One night Mr. Wizeman came into my room as I braced in front of Mr. Kaufman, helping him review for the next day's English quiz. The situation was ridiculous, with me bracing alone in the room, a frown on my face, while Mr. Kaufman made me pop off information about *Beowulf* so he wouldn't flunk the test. Mr. Wizeman was bright-eyed and cheerful that night, smiling as he listened to me spout trivia about Grendel and Grendel's mother for the quiz. I tried to maintain my stony expression, but over Mr. Kaufman's shoulder I could see Mr. Wizeman in a strange assortment of clothing: white shirt, PT shorts, Birkenstock sandals, and an ankle bracelet on one leg. I was notorious in my company for never cracking a smile at attention, but the sight of his grinning face, not to mention the sandals and ankle bracelet, was too much for me. I could feel my body tremble, and a moment later, I burst out laughing uncontrollably.

Mr. Wizeman gave me an exaggerated frown, accused me of making fun of his appearance, then turned to Mr. Kaufman and said, "Oh my gosh, that is the first uncontrollable laugh I have ever heard out of her! I was beginning to think I'd never hear one!"

Mr. Kaufman agreed, then yelled, "Gaudy knob, brace!" I made a smart about-face, brushed the tears from my cheeks, "wiped off" (wiped the smile from my face), and then turned back around and braced for Mr. Kaufman, my face once more set in a frown.

Mr. Wizeman shook his head ruefully and then remarked to Mr. Kaufman with a sigh, "This knob has no self-discipline." By the time he walked out the door a few moments later, I was once again reciting for Mr. Kaufman.

For weeks afterward, I was accused of being a "gaudy knob" by Mr. Wizeman. I think it became almost a challenge for him to break through my stone face. Almost no one could do it.

Bit by bit, I was gaining respect from other upperclassmen as well. Even one of the most strict upperclassmen let his guard down for short periods, asking me for advice on women. One night he asked me, Brooks, and Reich to start writing him letters, as he never got anything at mail call. I told him he was welcome to some of mine, but he just laughed and said no. A few days later, I got a note from him asking where his letters were. I knew he half meant it, and I suspected he was lonely, though he would never have admitted it. Relationships with upperclassmen were complicated for everyone involved. I had to walk a fine line between friendship and respect, for the boundary between the Fourth Class and the upper classes was sacred. Any personal relationship between male and female cadets was complicated. I'd done everything I could to protect myself from misunderstandings and rumors, promising myself not to date anyone during knob year. I'd asked my brother to take me to the one hop I'd attended. I knew a couple of my classmates wanted to date me, but dating would be like putting a target on my chest. I was already being called a slut; it would only get worse if I let myself get romantically involved with anyone in the Corps. The sexual harassment I'd undergone in high school had left a lasting mark on me.

Through all the challenges Mr. Wizeman remained my steady supporter. I respected him more than any other cadet in the Corps. Unlike so many others, he actually lived the ideals the college taught instead of just pretending to. In a thousand small ways, unnoticeable to anyone but me, he helped me gain confidence in myself. My mother nicknamed him my "guardian angel." Without crossing the boundary between upperclassman and knob, he kept watch over me in ways that were subtle but important. Three weeks after classes started, he assigned me to his personal "shine detail," ordering me to report to his quarters (or he would come to mine) every Sunday morning before Chapel to shine his brass. As I polished, he would talk to me about cadet life, letting me know indirectly how to survive. It was also his way of keeping an eye on me, of guaranteeing regular one-on-one contact between us. Perhaps most valuable, the weekly "Shine Duty" marked me as "his" knob, providing me with some protection from other upperclassmen who could have made my life a living hell. I came to rely on his watchful support.

And when I needed to talk with another woman, there were women I could turn to on campus. I found support and friendship in Dr. Zaremba, the faculty officer in charge of Special Services. She helped me cope with my ADD, advised me on how to get along with other cadets, and gave me an occasional shoulder to cry on when life in the Corps felt like too much. I was also getting to know Petra Lovetinska, the tall, tomboyish redhead who lived two doors down from me. Since Petra and I were in different companies, we hadn't had too much contact, but as the semester wore on, we both tried to spend more time together. Petra was funny and honest and loyal, and she worked hard to overcome her language barrier, which made classes difficult for her. She also had a great sense of humor, putting up with it good-naturedly when her cadre ordered her to make announcements on the PA system just so they could laugh at her Czech accent. Petra was no closer to Jeanie than I was to Kim, and we both wished we could room together.

In spite of the constant stress, life in the Corps wasn't all doom and gloom. In between the racking and marching, there were good times as well. One day at lunch mess, one of my classmates cleaned his plate, which was chicken—bones and all. We were all so astonished that we had to struggle not to stare. Even the mess carver couldn't believe it. Afterward, back in our rooms, my classmates and I laughed ourselves silly. The story soon became legendary. After all, who eats chicken bones?

Sometimes I even had fun with the fact that I was female. Since I couldn't help my gender, I thought I might as well have a sense of humor about it. I would intentionally put my bras in the front of the drawer for room inspection. Everything in the half-press had to be laid out according to a prescribed pattern, but the design didn't allow for female undergarments. The inspecting cadet officers never said a word about the bras, but I knew it made them uncomfortable. I also enjoyed keeping a large box of tampons and a pink blow dryer under the sink in my quarters. I didn't really need the blow dryer with my boy's haircut, but it was a symbolic gesture. I wanted to remind the male cadets that I might be a knob, but I was also a female. You didn't have to be one or the other. I even kept the little pink alarm clock I'd had since kindergarten on my desk. One cadet sergeant wanted me to heel and sole it, to make it look more military. Luckily for me, there was nothing against pink alarm clocks in the College rules.

One of the funniest incidents that fall happened directly because of my gender. I was running down the gallery toward the female latrine one night when Mr. Davis stopped me and demanded to know what was in the box I was carrying. I think he may have suspected I had a food package. Racking me the whole time, he snatched the package out of my grasp and ripped open the top. To his horror, tampons spilled out all over the ground. Completely losing his composure, Mr. Davis actually screamed and dropped the box, then rushed off across the quad. Shaking to control my laughter, I picked up the scattered tampons and returned to my room. Sometimes it was fun to be a girl.

And like college freshmen everywhere, we got caught up in the excitement of campus activities. At The Citadel, school spirit is raised to an art form, and knobs are in the big middle of it all.

One thing freshmen were responsible for was the school banners. The knobs had to provide banners for all major school events, and when I say banners, I don't mean a 4' by 6' piece of cloth run up a flagpole. Citadel banners are draped across the interior of a battalion, and we had to make them. We begged or borrowed or bought every flat white sheet we could lay our hands on until we had enough. Then we'd sew a half dozen of them together into a single banner, lay the whole thing out on the ground, and paint it Citadel blue with the slogan of the week. Many of the banners we made were more than twenty feet long. Decorating them was a messy job that usually resulted in stained PTs and needle marks in our fingers, but it was also really fun. Sometimes we'd go to my parents' house on weekends to get my mother's help with the sewing. My parents' driveway still has blue paint stains.

Friday lunch messes were another source of general insanity. Every Friday before a football game was scheduled, there would be a pep rally in the Mess Hall. An upperclass cadet referred to as the "twelfth man" (the so-called twelfth man on the football team) was in charge of the craziness. It was one of his jobs to act as the master of ceremonies at weekly pep rallies, but he reminded me more of a court jester. He usually arrived dressed in some ridiculous costume to rouse the "troops" to a fever pitch, preaching the "good word of The Citadel" like a country evangelist. We knobs were the cheering section. It was especially wild when we played VMI, for the schools had a rivalry that went back generations. On orders from the twelfth man, we braced on top of our chairs in the Mess Hall, then climbed down and marched around the tables, shouting in unison at the top of our lungs:

Are we going to beat VMI?

Hell Yes!

Is VMI going to beat us?

Hell No!

Well take a locomotive and take it slow

C-I-T-A-D-E-L

C-I-T-A-D-E-L

C-I-T-A-D-E-L

Yell Like Hell! CITADEL!

Hundreds of male voices—and four female—rose to a fever pitch as we shouted, our feet pounding in rhythm as they smacked the floor. On another order, our chant turned into a song, with the knobs expected to remember every word (to the tune of "The Army Goes Rolling Along"):

Give 'em hell, Citadel,

For it's down the victory trail.

As the Bulldogs go rolling along.

Hit 'em high, hit 'em low,

Never stop for any foe,

As the Bulldogs go rolling along.

For it's fight! Fight! Fight!

For the team in blue and white;

Shout out your spirit, loud and strong . . .

Still singing, we knobs would march out of the Mess Hall and down the road to our battalions. It was sheer pandemonium, and my small soprano voice got drowned in the deeper voices all around me, but I loved it. In those moments, no one even noticed that I was a girl.

Another knob activity was painting the boards, and even that was fun at times. Each barracks had large rectangles painted on the walls near the sally port, used as bulletin boards for the different companies. The Band Company boards were near the back sally port, and it was our job to paint them for special occasions. I would collect money from the other knobs to buy the materials; then our whole knob platoon would work together on the painting. Although we could only whisper to one another as we worked, the upperclassmen sometimes made us sing something ridiculous to entertain them as they supervised us. One day they ordered us to sing "Hi Ho, Hey Baby" while we painted. It sounded hilarious, and it was all I could do not to burst.

Somehow or other, the days passed, and October finally crept to an end. The fall winds were beginning to blow, and we changed from our summer leave uniform to our winter grays. It was midway through the semester, and I was still surviving, still strong, still determined to show what I was worth as a woman and a cadet.

As I ran down the gallery toward my room that last Friday in October, I heard a voice sounding off in the distance. It was Jeanie, trying her best to shout, her voice disappearing like a small leaf into the autumn wind. I smiled to myself, thinking, "Like mice, we shout, but our hearts are like tigers, strong!" As I reached the door to my quarters, I saw my classmate, Royal, a few yards ahead of me. He and several other knobs from my company were lined up, getting racked by Mr. Ingram. I had no idea what for. Without stopping to think, I kept running past my doorway, down to the end of the gallery where my classmates stood. Requesting permission to speak, I said, "Sir, Mr. Ingram, sir, Cadet Private Mace requests permission to join the formation, sir!" Then I took my place next to my classmates, braced, and felt Mr. Ingram's breath on my face as he moved down the row.

For the first time in my life, I almost enjoyed the racking. I wanted to be there with my classmates. After all, we were a team, weren't we?

★ CHAPTER 11 ★

HAIR OF
THE DOG

The first advice I'd been given when I was accepted at The Citadel was "try to blend in." Ghost knobs, as they are called, get the least harassment because they attract the least attention. Although I knew I could never blend in as a male would, I had worked hard to become "just another knob," drawing as little attention to myself as possible. Midway through the semester, I had finally become "invisible" to at least a few of my classmates, and I could walk across campus without everyone turning around to stare. That luxury ended abruptly, all because of the most trivial of issues: hair.

It don't know whose bright idea it was, but Kim and Jeanie, hoping to prove themselves "one of the boys," decided to demonstrate their solidarity by shaving off the back of their hair like the male knobs. Petra, as a member of the same company, felt obligated to follow their lead. The whole ridiculous scenario began in our room one night during ESP, when Kim and Jeanie came up with the notion. Their bright idea was to duplicate the male knobs' haircut by shaving off what remained of their own short hair. I was at the library studying when the discussion first started, and by the time I got back to our room, they were already shaving the bottom of their heads. Horrified, I told them they were crazy, and violating orders as well, but they had never had much interest in my opinion. Using the Bic razor Kim used to shave her legs, they took turns shaving the back of each other's heads. The result was horribly ugly, a butchered cut with nicks and patches of bare scalp showing through.

I was horrified and disgusted with the result, but they seemed pleased—so pleased, in fact, that they began pressuring me to follow their lead and shave off part of my own remaining hair. I refused, an argument followed, and eventually, they gave up and went in search of Petra. I thought Petra would have too much good sense to give in to them, but unfortunately, I was wrong. An hour later, Kim and Jeanie returned with Petra in tow, with M & M (as I'd nicknamed them) proudly displaying Petra's butchered scalp as proof of their united "courage." As they soon found out, I wasn't the only one who was disgusted by their actions. When they all tramped off to show their Echo Company cadet officers their "gesture of solidarity," they did not receive the welcome they expected. Instead, they got the racking of their lives and were hauled off to the Commandant's Office as fast as they could march. The colonel was equally horrified, as were the other administrators. The last thing the College needed was an "incident" with the female cadets for the papers to get hold of. Their fears were justified, for within twenty-four hours the news had hit the national wires, with front-page photos of Petra's shaved scalp in the Charleston papers and reports on every local television station. The implication behind all the media attention was that The Citadel was somehow responsible for making the three women feel "pressured" to fit in by destroying the last remnant of their femininity.

Just as unfairly, I found myself getting punished once again for my roommate's breach of conduct. In the days following the "incident," I was called into the Commandant's Office and made to endure the same scolding as the other three girls, even though I had refused to participate in their behavior. On Friday I was called into Captain Gay's office to discuss the incident with her, and I voiced my strong disapproval of what the other girls had done. As I saw it, it was a breach of cadet conduct, and a sign of immaturity. I told the captain that I had no desire to be "one of the boys," that I recognized and accepted the fact that I was different, and that my goal was to earn respect as a woman *and* a cadet, not as a "good old boy." I was proud of being female. I didn't want to be a male. She listened sympathetically and tried to console me, reassuring me that the administration did recognize my strength in declining to break the rules. Unfortunately, her words did little to relieve my frustration. I was worn down from the continual stress, and it was getting harder and harder to bounce back.

In a cruel twist of fate, I soon found that I was soon attracting more than my share of attention for my own haircut. It seemed to me that I had done my part by refusing to shave my head as the other girls had done, and by faithfully having my hair trimmed every Wednesday with the rest of Band Company. As things turned out, however, nothing I did seemed to satisfy my critics.

As I was returning to my battalion one afternoon shortly before Thanksgiving break, I heard my name called by Mr. Butler. I was accustomed to conversations with Mr. Butler, so I stopped and came to attention with no particular concern. To my astonishment, though, he immediately began racking me about my haircut. He informed me that an old gentleman on the Board of Visitors had seen me that morning and complained to the commandant that "that girl Mace" had too much hair. Asking permission to speak, I politely informed Mr. Butler that my hair was cut weekly to meet Citadel requirements. Mr. Butler did not seem impressed. He ordered me to return to the barber shop for another haircut.

So the next morning I made my way to the barber shop and explained that I had been told my hair was "too long." The barber, puzzled, trimmed the short fringe that remained on my head even shorter. My task completed, I reported to Mr. Butler, but when he saw the result, he remained dissatisfied. He told me that I still had "too much hair" for a knob, and ordered me to return to the barber shop to have my hair thinned. I couldn't believe what he was telling me. Most upperclass cadets, all of whom were male, had considerably more hair than I did at that moment, and I had never seen or heard of a cadet being ordered to have his hair *thinned*. I knew for a fact that my hair had already been trimmed "by the book," unlike that of the other three female knobs, who still looked like they'd collided with an electric razor. Swallowing my resentment, I replied, "Sir, yes, sir," and returned to the barber shop for the "thinning."

The sympathetic barber shook his head and dug out a pair of "thinning shears," but as he turned to begin the thinning process, something in me rebelled. All the emotions I'd held back for so long welled up, and

I lurched out of the chair before he could make the first snip, protesting, "No!" The tears were already beginning to spill over as I rushed out of the barber shop.

Word of my rebellion quickly reached Mr. Butler, who ordered me to report to Colonel Lackey's office for "discipline." I wiped the tears off my cheeks, pulled myself together, and made my way around the Parade Field, down the lane, and up the stairs to see the assistant commandant. Word of my insurrection had, I knew, already been relayed to the colonel. Taking a deep breath, I knocked and entered, then sat down across from the desk at the colonel's order. I was controlled by then, but stubbornly unrepentant. I knew my eyes were still red from crying, but I was determined not to lose my composure again.

Colonel Lackey asked me what had happened and listened politely to my somewhat impassioned defense of my actions. When I had finished, he sat quietly for a moment, then began to explain in a pleasant but firm voice what my options were. He told me that a longtime "friend of the school" had seen and objected to the amount of hair I was allowed to have as a knob. He acknowledged that thinning a cadet's hair was unusual, but pointed out that as knobs traditionally had their hair shaved off, this was the first time the "thickness" of a freshman's hair had been an issue. He finished by pointing out that the school thought it important to "respect" the wishes of its more dedicated alumni, as long as those wishes did not violate Corps policy. The order to thin my hair had not come from Mr. Butler; it had, in fact, come from "above the [Citadel] president." As a result, he was "asking" me to honor the administration's request that I thin my hair.

I sat there without speaking for a moment, staring over the colonel's shoulder, out the window behind his desk. It was clear that in spite of his careful phrasing, I had no real choice in the matter. My hair would have to be thinned, or I would be disciplined. All the injustices of the past three months paraded through my mind. I reflected bitterly for a moment that I was being treated as though I, like my female classmates, had somehow violated school haircut policy when in fact I had diligently followed procedure. The whole situation was grossly unfair. I was being asked to sacrifice what little remained of my femininity on the whim of some old geezer who probably thought women should still have to wear skirts. The question was, was I willing to go to the wall on this issue? Was it worth the price I would have to pay as a cadet?

As though reading my thoughts, Colonel Lackey quietly said, "You've always struck me as someone who picks her battles carefully, Mace. Is this one worth the fight?"

My eyes snapped back to his face. He was watching me intently. Taking a deep breath, I looked directly into his eyes and said, "I'm smarter than this, sir." Asking and receiving permission to be dismissed, I rose and said, "I will report to the barber shop immediately, sir." Saluting him, I walked out the door with my chin held high. After all, I reflected, it was only hair.

I had come to know myself, my strengths and my limitations, in a way I would not have thought possible even a month before. But it took an obstacle course—a literal one—to help me put a name to what drove me.

On the Monday before Thanksgiving, two of my company officers— Mr. Brooks and Mr. Uppole—took us knobs across campus to a training course I had never run before. Midway through it was a high obstacle that I had to scale in order to finish the course. I have always had a fear of falling from heights, and when I reached the top of the obstacle and was told to jump across, I panicked. As the cadets yelled, urging me on, I stood frozen on top, terrified and suddenly on the verge of tears. All I could think was that if I tried to jump, I would fall and hurt myself. Mr. Brooks and Mr. Uppole continued to shout encouragement, trying to motivate me to take the leap, yet even with their urging, it was several minutes before I found the courage to jump. I made it safely over, but afterward, the incident haunted me. What had I been so afraid of? I had always been an athlete, always had great physical courage. Why was this particular hurdle any different?

And then it hit me. It wasn't the falling I was so afraid of. It was the failure. The thought of failing in front of the Corps, of literally falling flat on my face as the men watched, was unbearably painful to me. I had put my whole life on the line in coming to The Citadel, all the pain and failures of the past, all my hopes for the future. No one, except possibly my mother, understood what my decision to come here meant to me. I had to succeed at this, or I would forever see myself as a failure. That night I wrote these words in my journal: "I am afraid to fail. If there is anything I fear most, I fear failure." That fear, I knew, was both my greatest strength and my greatest weakness. I would have to face that fear, or I would spend the rest of my life running from risks.

CHAPTER 12

PROMISES
TO KEEP

The long semester was wearing me down, both physically and mentally. The Citadel has always been notorious for the physical demands it makes on its knobs, and I was no exception. I had arrived that fall in the best physical shape of my life, but I sometimes felt that no amount of conditioning would be enough. A big part of it was simply keeping up with the males all around me. I could outdistance most of them in endurance, but the limitations of a female body meant I had to work three times as hard to equal them in strength. I knew that most cadets judged me primarily on my physical toughness, not my academic ability, and that meant I had to be perceived as the strongest of the strong physically if I wanted to be respected. It took all my discipline as an athlete to meet those expectations.

Piled on top of the other demands, the constant exercise was also exhausting. Basic PT was required of all knobs three times a week, after class on Mondays and Wednesdays at 1600, and after Parade on Fridays. It lasted for about an hour. We had to sign out in the battalion to ensure that we showed up. Once we formed up, we would be marched out to the athletic field for a minimum of thirty minutes of continual calisthenics, followed by a half hour of running. Tuesdays and Thursdays, we often participated in intramural sports, both to build our physical stamina and to encourage teamwork.

In the beginning I had enjoyed the PT, for it gave me a chance to shine. I'd worked hard at it, constantly setting new goals for myself, taking breaks during evening study period to do curls or work on diamond push-ups, determined to meet the male standards for upper body strength. Lately, though, it had become hard to keep up. The incessant demands of formation, marching, running laundry, Sweep Details, running the galleries, walking double time—all the daily demands of knob life—had left my body drained and often aching for rest. As November wore on, I became increasingly susceptible to colds, which further drained my energy.

And like all females who march in formation with males, I was in constant danger of developing pelvic stress fractures. Women's pelvises, designed to adjust for pregnancy, are inherently more vulnerable than males' to injury and dislocation. The real problem, though, lies with the difference in the length of women's legs. Marching pace and cadence are set in accordance with the length of the average male's legs. Since women's legs are usually shorter, keeping step with males means constantly stretching the pelvis to accommodate the longer male stride. Hours of drilling, day in and day out, can lead to hairline fractures of the female pelvis, painful and potentially serious if not properly attended to. Both Kim and Jeanie had been sidelined with stress fractures, and I was regularly sent to the infirmary for pain in the pelvic area. Fortunately, my years of swimming paid off, and I never suffered anything more serious than a strain.

Lack of sleep was also becoming a serious problem for me. I was sleeping less and less, both from the insomnia of constant stress and the demands of studying. It got so bad for a couple of weeks that I considered asking for sleeping pills. My roommate's late night adventures sometimes made the problem intolerable. On the worst nights, I would go to Petra's room at two or three in the morning and crawl in Jeanie's empty bunk for what remained of the night. One morning, after being kept up all night by Kim and Jeanie's playing on the computer, I ended up in Dr. Zaremba's office, crying from sheer exhaustion. She gave me an excuse for my morning class and stuck me in an empty office in Student Services. I pulled a folding chair up to the dusty table, put my head down on my arms, and fell fast asleep. At that moment I could have slept on an Air Force runway.

The physical toll was obvious to anyone who looked at me. A photograph of my platoon taken that month shows me pale and thin in the front row, my eyes dark and serious, the bones of my face outlined, the circles under my eyes dark and puffy. I'd lost seven pounds in the first two weeks of school, and my weight was continuing to drop, reaching a dangerous low. A cadet I hardly knew even came up to me one day to say he was worried about me, that I needed to eat. I knew that rumors were circulating that I was anorexic. It wasn't true, but the starchy meals in the Mess Hall did not offer the nutrition needed by my overworked metabolism. I'd volunteered for an extra PT the second week of November because my weight was too low to give blood for the campus blood drive. The minimum weight for a woman to remain in the Corps was 98 pounds. At 5'5" tall, my weight hovered precariously at 99 pounds, and I had begun going to the infirmary for mandatory weight checks. My whole body hurt, from the blisters on my heels to the ache in the small of my back. But the worst ache that chilly November was the one in my heart.

The haircutting incident had focused the Corps' attention on us women once more, reviving the contempt we'd endured in the very beginning. After two months of eating, drilling, and sleeping alongside our male counterparts, we women had finally begun to blend into the scenery a bit, but the hair disaster focused attention on us all over again. The media scrutiny was especially damaging, for many of the news articles implied the male cadets were to blame.

The result was that all four of us were racked with renewed passion. It became difficult for me to even walk across campus without being stopped and racked by some stranger. On my way back to the battalion after class one afternoon, a cadet I had never seen before ordered me to halt and brace, then proceeded to tell me that I was a "worthless shitbag." In a voice low enough not to carry to passersby, he told me that I might be getting by in "Queer Company," but that in any other company I would just be another shitbag who wouldn't have made it through the first week. Biting the inside of my lip to maintain control, I had no choice but to respond, "Sir, yes, sir," to his stream of insults. When he finally released me, I trotted toward the barracks trembling with anger.

The worst times were at night, when I had to walk across campus alone, to or from the library or museum, where I would go to do research. As I walked down the street in front of the battalions, anonymous voices would ring out from darkened galleries and open windows. "Whore!" I would hear echoing through the darkness. "Dyke!" "Get out of our school!" "We know who you are! We'll make sure you don't make it!" There was a menacing quality to those moments that disturbed me. "No fear," I would tell myself. "No fear." I would walk steadily on, eyes straight ahead, clutching the handle of my book bag, until I emerged from the shadows into the light of the library or my own barracks. I didn't think any of them would really hurt me physically, for discipline is tight in the Corps. There are other kinds of pain, though, that are just as bad.

One night my mother met me in the library to bring me some materials I needed, and I told her I had been stopped several times on the way. The echoing taunts had been followed by two random rackings from cadets I had encountered en route. The five-minute trip from the battalion to the library had taken me nearly twenty minutes to complete, for someone kept stopping me to tell me how worthless I was. I reassured my mother that the threats were harmless, that I felt physically safe on campus, but I could tell that the situation bothered her. I couldn't blame her. It bothered me, too. Do you ever get used to being told you're worthless? I couldn't seem to. It wasn't the words that bothered me. I had become hardened to foul language. It was the fact that the other cadets meant them that was so painful.

The lowest point of the semester came for me in mid-November. I remember the incident like it was yesterday. I was walking alone toward the library, along the gutter of the Avenue of Remembrance that borders the Parade Field. The Avenue of Remembrance is sacred in Citadel lore, for it honors the lives of those who have given their lives for their country, dedicated their lives to the College, or both. General Clark's grave and monument lie along the Avenue, as does Summerall Chapel, dedicated to the memory of Citadel cadets. For these reasons, only upperclassmen—who have already proven their worthiness to be cadets—are allowed to walk on the sidewalk of the Avenue. Freshman walk only in the gutter, inside the line painted two feet from the curb. In the winter, the gutter is often filled with water. Wet feet are considered a small sacrifice for knobs to make as a show of respect.

As I hurried down the gutter toward the library for evening study period, I heard a cadet's voice ring out from the rear, ordering me to halt. The voice was vaguely familiar, but I couldn't quite place it. I began to do an about-face, but the voice abruptly ordered me to stop and brace. The voice continued talking to me softly, coming closer and closer until I could see a shadow from the corner of my eye on the curb behind me. Leaning forward until I could feel his breath on the back of my neck, he began to rack me in an insidious, threatening manner. "You are a shitbag, you know that, Mace? I have no respect for you. I know who you are. I know all about your history, and you are a piece of shit. When are you going to quit? I have learned everything I need to know about you. I know where you came from, and what you did. I hate you, do you hear me? I hate you!" I swallowed roughly, trying not to choke on my own saliva. I didn't say a word, and I didn't turn around. He leaned even further in, until I could smell his perspiration. Then he said with pointed emphasis, every word a stab, "You-are-a-piece-of-shit! Leave-my-school!" And with that, he walked away. I never saw his face.

When his footsteps finally echoed into silence, I began walking rapidly back toward my battalion. My cheeks were burning and I was flooded with nausea, but I kept my head high and my eyes straight ahead as I covered the endless steps back to the front sally port and around the corner to my quarters. Over and over I murmured to myself, "Shitbag, shitbag, shitbag." My face was set in stone, and I bit the inside of my cheek until I drew blood to keep the tears back. I closed my hands to keep them from shaking. I made it all the way back to the battalion without being stopped, and only when the door was closed behind me did I cry. Thank God, for once my roommate wasn't there.

Hands still shaking, I picked up my journal and began to write: "I hate this place! I hate this place! I hate every fucker in it!" I knew what he had heard about me, what they had all heard. The old lies still stalked me, like an obsessed lover. I couldn't seem to leave them behind; the harder I tried, the more they grew. I put my head down on the desk and tried to calm my breathing. Maybe he hadn't heard those stories. Maybe he'd made up new ones. Did it even matter anymore? Despair washed over me like a wave.

That night when Kim returned with Jeanie in tow to "play" some more on the computer, I slipped into my PT's and crept down the gallery to Petra's room. Curled up in Jeanie's empty rack, I began to cry once more. I sobbed much of the night. Petra hugged me and, sensing I didn't want to talk, crawled into her own rack and turned off the lights. I just couldn't face another night with Kim's hostility in the room. There was too much hostility outside that room already. The next morning, chin high, I washed my face and fell into line with the others. Nothing, nobody was going to make me quit. For me, failure would be a kind of death, the death of every hope I had for self-respect. I had set my face in stone. I would never look back.

When human comfort wasn't enough, I turned to God. I had attended chapel faithfully from my first weekend on campus, and as the days darkened, I came to rely more and more on the spiritual solace I found there. Formal Sunday morning service at Summerall Chapel is a singularly beautiful event, symbolizing the best of The Citadel with a moving blend of Christian and military ritual.

The inscription over the Chapel doorway reads, REMEMBER NOW THY CREATOR IN THE DAYS OF THY YOUTH, and the moment you enter the building, designed in the shape of a cross, your eyes are drawn to the gorgeous display of stained glass behind the altar. The giant window, constructed of jewel-toned glass, is a monument to all Citadel graduates who have died in the service of their country. The designs and figures symbolize courage, sacrifice, religion, truth, duty, loyalty, patriotism, faith, charity, prayer, adoration, praise, and immortality—an accurate list of the College's priorities. Underneath lies this inscription:

To the Glory of God
and in memory of
The Citadel's patriotic dead
this window is enshrined.

It is impossible to sit in that chapel without thinking of eternity, without an awareness of the generations of cadets who sat in those same pews and later laid down their lives on the fields of Iwo Jima or Vietnam. The common concerns of everyday life seem to drop away in the face of such solemn reminders. Each Sunday that November, dressed in my gray uniform, I sat with other members of my company in the lovely cruciform building where generations of cadets had worshipped before me. In those moments, the divisions and hostilities fell away in the presence of our common Creator.

The service always began with an organ prelude and the Posting of the Colors by the Chapel Color Guard. Six cadets in dress uniform, two of them carrying large, the brilliant United States and Christian flags, marched down the aisle in lock step to the cadence of their commander. The only sound in the sanctuary was the tap, tapping of the soles of dress shoes, with the voice of the young cadet occasionally punctuating the rhythm. All six would come to a stop at the steps leading to the altar, then two by two, make their way up the steps to place the flags in their holders under the chancery window. The vivid scarlet and gilt of the flags reflected the tints of the glass backdrop. In a series of crisp facings and marching in place, knees lifted to waist level, the Color Guard then reversed its movements, down the steps and down the aisle, again accompanied only by the echo of their own footsteps. The effect was solemn, almost haunting.

The singing of hymns and the scripture readings that followed were drawn from the traditional liturgy of Protestant Christianity. I liked to watch Mr. Wizeman as he sang each week in the Chapel Choir. It comforted me. Halfway through the service, the entire Corps rose as one to recite the Cadet Prayer:

Almighty God, the source of life and strength, we implore Thy blessing on this our beloved institution, that it may continue true to its high purposes.

Guide and strengthen those upon whom rests the authority of government; enlighten with wisdom those who teach and those who learn; and grant to all of us that through sound learning and firm leadership, we may prove ourselves worthy citizens of our country, devoted to truth, given to unselfish service, loyal to every obligation of life and above all to Thee.

Preserve us faithful to the ideals of The Citadel, sincere in fellowship, unswerving in duty, finding joy in purity, and confidence through a steadfast faith.

Grant to each one of us, in his own life, an humble heart, a steadfast purpose, and a joyful hope, with a readiness to endure hardship and suffer if need be, that truth may prevail among us and that Thy will may be done on earth.

Sunday after Sunday I would sit there, the prayer echoing through my mind, and draw strength from the stillness of those moments. "Endure hardship." Yes, I could do that, as my father had done before me. As thousands of other cadets had done before me. I would look up at the beautiful panes of glass shining above the altar. Each represented a different aspect of courage. The cadets whose names were listed next to them had shown the ultimate courage: They had faced death for something they believed in. I would look at Mr. Wizeman's kind, handsome face as he sat quietly in the choir box. I could do this, I reflected. Mr. Wizeman would see me graduate. I had promised myself that, and I never went back on a promise.

CHAPTER 13

HOLIDAY BLUES

For three and a half months, I had dreamed of December and the long, lazy days that awaited me at month's end. I knew that if I could just survive final exams and a few more weeks of military training, my reward would be home-cooked meals and long afternoon naps in the quiet of my own room. I could hardly wait. Exhausted as I was, I felt certain that the worst of the semester was over. As usual, I was wrong. A season that began with celebration and joy would end in chaos for the entire campus.

The holiday season was already upon us. Thanksgiving was only a few days away, followed shortly by finals and Christmas break. All around me, the campus was beginning to reflect the year's decline and the beginning of the holiday season. Holidays at The Citadel were a welcome relief from the constant harassment of freshman year, for even at El Cid, holidays were occasions to celebrate.

At Halloween three weeks earlier, the knobs had been responsible for decorating the battalion and providing treats. I had taken Alex home with me to my parents' house on leave one Saturday, where we'd carved a whole pile of pumpkins into jack-o'-lanterns to take back to the barracks. I'd also collected money for candy, and with some extra money my parents threw in, Alex and I had come back to campus with an impressive sack of goodies. On Halloween night, the seniors dressed up and came trick-or-treating to the knobs' rooms. I spent the hours after dark handing out candy with the other knobs in my platoon. Three of us shoved a half-press across the doorway of another knob's room and barricaded ourselves behind it, throwing candy at the seniors and ducking for cover. Naturally, we all got racked, but even the racking was good-natured, and nobody wrote me up for punishment.

Halloween Mess was especially cool, because for once, we were allowed to have a little fun at dinner. Instead of having me pop off my usual Mess Fact, the mess carver ordered me to scare my food. At first I told him I couldn't, but when he ordered me again, I looked down at my plate and then shrieked at the top of my lungs. Everyone at our table jumped out of their skins, even the mess carver. It was hilarious. I had to take a drink of water to keep the cadets from noticing the smirk on my face. Then Clark, the knob who was helping me serve that night, leaned down over his plate and yelled at his food, too. By then everyone at our table was laughing so hard they couldn't eat, and people started coming from other tables to see what was going on. They thought maybe the knobs were getting hazed or something. When the other cadets asked who had screamed, everyone pointed at Clark. We all burst out laughing again, and the others walked away, shaking their heads.

Afterward, Clark and I were ordered to tell a scary story, so we took turns making one up. Clark started it, then I continued, then Clark, and so on, all the way to the end. I finished the story by saying I had eaten the hearts of upperclassmen and thrown them up in a trash can, where they'd turned into maggots and been served in the Mess Hall for dinner. Then I pointed to the pasta we were eating and said, "Look, there they are!" Naturally, I'd made sure to mention the names of all five upperclassmen sitting at our table when I pointed at the "maggots." Those five fine gentlemen all doubled over laughing and rewarded me and Clark with apple pie for dessert. Freshmen *never* got pie. The whole evening was amazing.

After the stress of the previous weeks, I was looking forward to Thanksgiving as a time to relax and celebrate a little. By the week after Halloween, the knobs were already planning the next holiday event. I knew some of my officers loved Girl Scout cookies, so I e-mailed my mom to ask her if she could possibly lay her hands on a few boxes of the chocolate mints. If a few cookies would get the platoon sergeant to ease up on us a bit, I was all for it. I was also tasked with gathering the "props" our company upperclassmen wanted for Thanksgiving Mess. My duties included buying the cigars that the cadets at our mess table planned to smoke in honor of the occasion, as well as gathering a list of materials for decorations and costumes. We all threw ourselves into the preparations with enthusiasm, even though it meant memorizing special "Thanksgiving Mess Facts" and gathering a long list of props. It was a welcome relief from academics and military training.

For 360 days a year, El Cid is the strictest, most disciplined college campus in the United States—"Alcatraz on the Ashley," as the grads call it. On celebration days, however, watch out! All that energy we had to bottle up the rest of the year came bursting out. Thanksgiving Mess was the beginning of a night of sheer, unbridled insanity.

My classmates and I had spent hours doing arts and crafts to prepare for the big occasion. We arrived early at the Mess Hall to decorate our mess table with fancy paper place mats decorated with turkeys and Pilgrims. I'd cut out a picture of a bottle of Wild Turkey whiskey, and I taped it to the pitcher of iced tea. Apparently the picture was enough motivation, for everyone chugged ice tea and carried on during evening mess as though they really were drunk. We'd also provided Thanksgiving hats for everyone at the mess table. My classmates made me a paper headpiece and nicknamed me "Mayflower" for the evening, and we each made a special "hat" for our upperclassmen to wear at dinner, with a name to match. Mr. Norris was "Mr. Beefeater," with SMEGMA written across the front of a tiny little Pilgrim hat less than three inches in diameter. Mr. Albayade had a big cowboy hat with a clown taped on front, making him the "clown prince" of the mess table. I had spent hours on an Indian headdress for Mr. Thaxton, using real pheasant and turkey feathers, and everyone agreed he looked incredibly cool. We named him "Chief Hunts Things." He seemed pleased with my hard work and even kept the hat on after dinner.

Released for the evening from our usual restrictions, we knobs stuffed ourselves with turkey and trimmings and several pieces of pie. Famished and relaxed, I ate until I burst and still felt hungry. Just for the one meal, we were allowed to eat without bracing, and we took full advantage of the opportunity. Laughing so hard we spit our food back out on the table, we listened as our classmates recited "Creative Mess

Facts" they had chosen for the occasion. I solemnly recited the history of Girl Scout cookies, every trace of a smile wiped off my face as I sounded off. Every now and then, a cadet officer would ask us a question, but instead of "Sir, yes, sir," we were instructed to reply, "Yo, man," which sent everyone into further fits of hysterics. I was even allowed to say, "Yeah, dude," in reply to questions, which made everyone laugh even more. By the end of the meal, my stomach ached from laughter and extra food.

Afterward, the knobs passed out the cigars we had been asked to buy for everyone, and we lit up and went back to the battalion together for an after-hours party. All the knobs met in Mike Alpaugh's room for a smoke-out dance party. Mike painted himself with highlighter and turned on a black light. He looked amazing, the highlighter marks glowing eerily when he moved. Someone cranked up the stereo and we all started screaming and dancing, still smoking our cigars. One of my classmates started a dance chain, up the chair, onto the desk, and across the half-press to the rack. I followed along, cigar dangling out of the left side of my mouth like my father, removing it only long enough to join in the singing.

After a while, upperclassmen started filtering in to join the fun, and I found myself dancing on a chair with a long string of classmates and cadet officers alike. Suddenly, I realized for the first time being the only girl in the company was a very good thing. The room filled with smoke, and when the CD ran out, I turned toward the corner and shouted, "Turn the freaking music on!" Too late I realized that Mr. Thaxton was the one at the stereo, and for a moment I froze with embarrassment. Everyone got quiet and looked from Mr. Thaxton to me, but after a moment's surprise, he just shoved the turkey feather headpiece down farther on his head and put on another CD. Everyone burst out laughing. I was dizzy with happiness and relief.

When the smoke got so thick we couldn't stand it in the room, we all dragged a mattress outside and went "sledding" on the quad. I went sliding across the forbidden red and white squares with my classmates, howling with laughter. I remember looking up for a moment and seeing Mr. Dye, just standing there and watching us with amazement. For once, he didn't rack us, but I couldn't help wondering what in the world he was thinking. It was as though all of us knobs had simply lost our minds for a few hours. People were snapping pictures left and right. I raced back to my room for my own camera. This was a night I wanted to have on film.

When All-In sounded at 2300, no one wanted to go to bed. As I peeled off my uniform and pulled on my pajamas, I thanked my lucky stars that I hadn't worn my contacts that night. The smoke would have ruined them. In cadet language, I would have been an SOL ("Shit Out of Luck"!). I reeked of cigars, and my eyes burned and watered. I would have killed for a shower, but that would have to wait until morning. I couldn't believe the night that had just passed. I had never spoken to an upperclassman so disrespectfully in my life as I had spoken to Mr. Thaxton, yet for that one short evening, no one had seemed to mind. My throat hurt from screaming, but I felt more relaxed than I had since Hell Week began. I wondered what my parents would have thought if they'd seen me dancing with that cigar. I'd have a great story to tell when I got home.

Lying in bed, too excited to go right to sleep, my eyes filled with tears of joy. "I love this place," I thought, "I really do. Even though every day is a bad day, I love it anyway. And the guys do respect me. Most of them really do. Halfway through, halfway through, I'm halfway through to May." I knew I would remember this night forever. I was still smiling as I drifted off to sleep.

My good mood lasted all the way through the following week. After four days at home to eat, sleep, and play, I returned to the battalion at the end of November happy and refreshed. With finals two weeks away, I buckled down for the final push toward A's in my classes. The barracks were relatively quiet as other cadets also settled in to study and work on papers. I had visitors asking for help with accounting nearly every night. I liked helping the upperclassmen; it made me feel useful, even respected. When my nineteenth birthday rolled around on December 4, I didn't even mind spending it on campus. My mother sent me a care package filled with goodies, and my family—and even a few of my classmates— sent me happy birthday wishes. I made a mental note to e-mail my father on his birthday the following week.

Christmas was coming soon as well, and that meant it was time for the knobs to collect money for decorations. Each year the cadets covered the battalions with Christmas lights, thousands of them, until the barracks sparkled like magic castles. All seventeen companies competed with each other for the best decorations, to be judged by Citadel administrators and faculty, and the competition was fierce. I collected over $150 from my classmates, and my mother went out and bought dozens of light strings, adding a few of her own for good measure. I counted the total before we hung them: 6,300 miniature lights. It was amazing. We knobs spent hours planning where to put them. We hung them from the galleries, from the overhangs, from the windows, even wrapped the columns in sparkling red and white to look like candy canes. It took us nearly a week to finish, working afternoons and every night before and after evening formation.

I don't know whether it was the exhaustion or the holidays, but as December wore on, I found it harder and harder to keep the solemn expression I'd worn all semester. I'd long had a reputation in my company as "Stone Face," for I'd learned to hide my emotions behind a serious mask. Now I was having trouble wiping a grin off my face. One evening while we were stringing Christmas lights, Reich and I got the bright idea of taping the sergeants' door closed from the outside with duct tape. We made our escape successfully, but later at formation, Reich got the giggles. I guess it was just nerves, but for some reason, he couldn't stop laughing. I could feel his shoulder shaking where it pressed against mine, and the laughter was contagious. Soon I was shaking uncontrollably as well. Our sergeant, Mr. Pappas, immediately ordered us to about-face and "wipe off," meaning to wipe the smiles off our faces. We did as he ordered, but no sooner did we turn around than Brooks, standing on the other side of me, also started to laugh. That did it. Reich and I were goners. All three of us doubled over, howling uncontrollably, tears running down our faces. Mr. Pappas asked us what was so funny, and I tried to say, "Sir, no excuse, sir," but my voice cracked, and that made me laugh even harder. Then Mr. Pappas told us to pop off some Knob Knowledge as punishment, and I got the bright idea of popping off the Pledge of Allegiance. All the knobs joined in, popping off the Pledge in rhythm. Mr. Pappas frowned and yelled even harder, but it did no good. It was all we could do to pull ourselves together for the march to evening mess. No amount of racking made us stop.

After mess, Mr. Pappas ordered us to report to his room for punishment. The three of us lined up and braced as Mr. Pappas spelled out our punishment. We would be confined to our quarters until we had written SIR, MR. PAPPAS, SIR, THIS CADET PRIVATE WILL NOT FREAKIN' LAUGH, SIR! one hundred times. After racking us some more, he dismissed us to our quarters to complete our assignment. We shook with laughter all the way there. Fortunately, I was able to put on my stone face long enough to turn in my "written assignment." Not that it helped in the long run. The next day we got the giggles all over again.

Later that week, in a surprising burst of holiday spirit, our platoon sergeant, Mr. Dye, actually decided to help Evan Reich celebrate Hanukkah. Because Reich was the only Jew in our platoon, there was no one to share the traditional Hebrew celebration with him. On the first morning of Hanukkah, Mr. Dye sent a notice around inviting the Band Company knobs to come to Evan's room for the lighting of the menorah. Since it was a religious celebration, Mr. Dye could not require us to attend, but Evan was touched by the kind gesture. Evan e-mailed everyone, too, telling us that he would teach us how to play driedel, the traditional Hanukkah game, as well. That night Brooks and I and a dozen or so other knobs gathered in Evan's room with Mr. Dye for the candle lighting ceremony. Wearing his yarmulke, the traditional hat worn by Jews during religious services, Evan recited the appropriate prayer in Hebrew and lighted the first candle in the menorah he had brought from home. I watched solemnly as Evan completed the ancient ritual. When he finished, there was a moment of silence; then Mr. Dye asked Evan to translate the prayer into English for the rest of us. There was an even longer silence before Evan finally confessed that he couldn't remember. He knew all the Hebrew words. He had learned them for his bar mitzvah six years before. He just couldn't remember exactly what they meant. The poor guy blushed and looked pretty sheepish as Mr. Dye just said, "Oh," and walked out of the room. The rest of us burst out laughing and sat down to play driedel for pennies.

Naturally, the holiday atmosphere was too good to last. The middle of December brought the Corps the biggest scandal since Shannon Faulkner had left The Citadel a year before. As the second week of December drew to a close, the shit hit the fan like a hurricane off Charleston Harbor.

Many of us at The Citadel who knew Kim and Jeanie had been predicting trouble for months. They didn't seem particularly interested in their classes and had been written up for sloppiness and absence from formation. By November, Petra and I were "covering" for our roommates' shortcomings almost daily. We each did the work of two people in our rooms, or none of us would have passed inspection. And when Kim and Jeanie came back from a weekend leave too drunk to stand and threw up all over themselves, it was Petra and I who saw that they made it to formation. That evening I had to clean the vomit out of the sink and we had to hold them upright while we dressed them in their uniforms like rag dolls.

Soon Kim began asking me to hide things because she said she was having "problems." First it was a sweatshirt, then notes and other articles of clothing. She refused to tell me exactly what was going on. When I asked her if she had reported these problems to her chain-of-command, she gave me a vague answer. When I offered to speak to the proper authorities myself, she said she'd think about it. The whole thing made me uneasy. I wondered what in the world was going on.

Ten days after my birthday, the storm descended. Appropriately, it was Friday the thirteenth. I was on my way back to the battalion after morning classes when the rumor first reached me. M&M (as I had nicknamed Messer and Mentlavos) had filed charges against The Citadel, claiming hazing and sexual harassment, including being set on fire by Echo Company cadet officers. I couldn't believe what I was hearing. Within hours, the campus turned into a zoo, with media helicopters overhead, reporters swarming everywhere, and all branches of law enforcement—campus, city, state, and federal—descending at once. It was as if the whole world had suddenly gone insane.

I was one of the very first people ordered to report to the President's Office. As Kim's roommate and "keeper of the evidence," I was the center of intense questioning by the FBI and other law enforcement groups. I turned over everything Kim had given me and answered their questions as honestly as I could. Finally, they asked me if my chain-of-command officers had subjected me to the kind of hazing that Kim and Jeanie reported. I replied that they had not, that except for some nasty comments, my company had treated me like all the other knobs. After hours of questioning, I was finally dismissed. The first thing I did was to call my mother and reassure her that I was all right.

Kim did not return to our room that night, or the night after. On Monday I was told that she would be taking her final exams on schedule but would not be returning to the barracks. She and Jeanie were being housed off campus and would return only under guard and in civilian clothes. The Echo Company cadets named in the complaint had already been suspended, and the entire company put under lock down. None of them were allowed to leave, except for classes and necessary military duty. I was asked to pack up Kim's belongings for her. I put her clothing and books in boxes and took her computer apart for transfer. A few hours later, someone came by to pick them up.*

With the authorities called in and rumors spreading like wildfire, security was increased around Petra and me. Guards were set, and we were ordered to lock our doors at night. Panic buttons that would immediately summon the guards were installed in our rooms, and each of us was given a cellular phone so that we could call for help in an emergency. Adult tactical officers were quartered in our barracks at night. Colonel Trez came by personally to ask me and Petra if we felt safe. We both assured him that we did. Even my brother James was worried and e-mailed me to make sure I'd made it safely through the weekend. I told him I was fine, but I was touched that he cared. I felt perfectly safe. Everyone was looking out for me.

Final exams, on the other hand, were hell. I desperately wanted to finish the semester with A's, but it was hard to concentrate in the midst of all the chaos. The college didn't dare ban reporters from campus for fear of being charged with a cover-up. The whole thing was a public relations nightmare for the school, and I suddenly found myself the center of very unwelcome attention. I couldn't walk anywhere on campus without being chased by someone with a camera. On Monday I literally ran several blocks from the fieldhouse to my barracks, sprinting through

---

* Kim Messer and Jeanie Mentlavos, two of the first class of women to enter The Citadel in August 1996, left after one semester. Both sued the college, alleging verbal and physical abuse. While admitting no guilt, The Citadel settled out of court with a monetary payment to both plaintiffs.

the front sally port to avoid TV news reporters in hot pursuit.

Wednesday of finals week was the worst. I encountered the full media onslaught on my way to Capers Hall for my English final. Lined up on the sidewalk were elbow-to-elbow reporters, with news vans and cameras parked nearby, sprouting antennae like strange insects. From yards away, someone spotted me, shouting, "Look! It's one of the girl cadets!" and soon cries of "It's Nancy Mace, the roommate!" echoed all around me. Like a tidal wave, they descended on me in a mass. My impulse was to turn and run for the barracks, where I would be safe once inside, but I couldn't. I had a final exam to complete. Taking a deep breath, I put on my stone face and walked straight ahead, eyes straight ahead, ignoring the chaos all around me. Ironically, the nonstop racking I'd endured for three months had taught me to ignore even the most extreme invasion of my personal space. Ignoring the rising hysteria all around me, I made my way steadily through the crowd and into the relative safety of Capers Hall with a sigh of relief. My cheeks were burning. I felt like a trapped animal, longing for escape.

For weeks, I had dreamed of home, but when I got a chance to leave campus early, I jumped at the offer. The moment I completed my last final, I packed up in record time and caught a ride with Alex and a senior cadet who offered to give us a lift to his house. Alex's mother and sister picked us up there and drove us to Alex's home in Georgia. The relief I felt at getting off campus was overwhelming. Dressed in civilian clothes, nobody would recognize me there. I was desperate to be anonymous, to walk down the street without being bothered, something that had become impossible in Charleston.

After two days in Georgia and several conversations with my

parents, I decided to accept my Auntie Beth's offer to spend Christmas with her family in Florida. Mom and Dad arranged for my ticket, and Alex and his mother drove me to the Atlanta airport for the flight to Florida. They very kindly offered to stay with me at the gate until it was time to board, but I told them I'd be fine, that I really just wanted a little time alone to rest and make some phone calls. Alex's mother gave me a hug and wished me Merry Christmas, and they both walked away.

I perched on the edge of the vinyl seat, my carry-on bag at my feet. It was chaos all around me, with loudspeakers paging passengers and holiday crowds rushing to greet loved ones or make their own flights. Hundreds of people hurried past me, and not one of them gave me a second glance. They had no idea who I was. I smiled and sat back in the seat. It was the most peaceful moment I'd had in two weeks.

★ CHAPTER 14 ★

STAR
PERFORMER

There is no such thing as "getting over the hump" at The Citadel. When I returned for the final semester of my knob year, I knew I was facing another four months of hell. At least it would be a familiar hell this time.

From the first day I set foot back on campus, it was difficult. I found my room filled with Kim's lawyers, gathering evidence for her lawsuit against the school. The handful of cranky upperclassmen in the battalion outside seemed to think this was my fault. I was thrilled to receive my first grade report, but then at my first formation I was racked because I had "only gotten" a 3.75 grade point average. With only twelve units, I was told, I should have gotten a 4.0. The guy next to me, on the other hand, who had squeaked by with a 1.8 average (and twelve units as well), was hardly racked at all. I kept a stone face but murmured curse words in my head while they made fun of me. They had no idea how hard it was for me to make good grades with a learning disability. It was a painfully sensitive subject.

Afterward, I was called in to Colonel Leedom's office and told I would have to be deposed in a judge's chambers about what had happened to Kim and Jeanie. "Great," I thought, "Kim's finally gone, but she's still making my life miserable." It was not a good way to start the semester.

Things got even worse the second week, in a way I didn't expect. I was used to being harassed by upperclassmen, but my company classmates and I were a team. I could depend on them—or so I thought. One evening in early January, I went to the squad room with Reich and Brooks as usual, to plan our next knob project. The room was crowded with the knobs in our platoon, and every time I tried to say something, some of the guys started to laugh. I couldn't understand it. After a few minutes, I got embarrassed and left.

Later that evening, I went to Reich and Brooks's room to ask them what was going on. I could tell they were uncomfortable and didn't want to tell me. Finally, Allyn explained that while I was talking, another knob had stood behind me and simulated having sex with me from the rear. I was mortified and furious. It was high school all over again. I could feel the tears stinging my eyes. Both Evan and Brooks felt terrible about what had happened and did their best to comfort me. They told me that I should go to my chain-of-command, and that they would back me up.

I went to our classmates frst to try to work it out with them without going up the chain-of-command. They denied everything. When that attempt failed, we went to our squad sergeant, Mr. Schuler, and told him what had happened. Mr. Schuler was furious and racked both the and racked both the cadet and his roommate for behavior "unbecoming a cadet." He also pointed out that what they had done to me was sexual harassment, which was illegal. They kept their mouths shut while Mr. Schuler was in the room, but an hour later, one of the cadets came to my quarters privately and told me what happened with Schuler and called me a "fucking liar." When I told Mr. Schuler what had happened, he promised to take the matter to the next level of the chain-of-command. Both cadets were punished, and eventually they came to me and apologized. The damage had been done, though. It was a long time before I felt comfortable with my classmates again.

Some things did get better the second half of the semester. As the only two remaining females, Petra and I were finally allowed to room together. I also decided to "roach" (apply) for company clerk for the following year, a highly competitive position of honor, and I had high hopes of being chosen. I began to roach for the current clerks—which meant I ran errands and helped out as a way of proving myself and of learning the job. I kept telling myself that if I worked hard enough, my achievements would be recognized, and the Corps would have to respect me. "When you're eating an elephant," my mother had told me, "you just have to take it one bite at a time." I just got a little tired of all that chewing at times.

The early weeks of 1997 were an odd mixture of pain and joy. I was happy to be back, happy to be with my friends and recognize how far we had come, yet every day remained a "bad day" of some sort. I hadn't admitted it to anyone, but in my heart I was desperately hoping to see my name on the Commandant's List at the end of January. The Commandant's List names the best cadets from each company, academically and militarily, who have made the biggest contribution during the semester. One afternoon Mr. Dye came to see me in my quarters, and I couldn't figure out why. Out of all the upperclassmen, Mr. Dye had racked me the hardest all·semester, and I feared him greatly. This time, though, he chatted about unimportant matters and seemed kind of nervous. After a few minutes, he began to ask me about my family, saying he'd heard that my father was a grad. I replied that he was, with a "sir sandwich" (wedging my response between "sir's").

Finally, Mr. Dye asked me if I knew what the Commandant's List was. I felt my heart leap into my throat as I answered, "Sir, yes, sir." Then he told me that the List had just been posted on the board and asked me if I'd seen the name of the best knob in Band Company. My stomach filled with butterflies of hope and curiosity as I answered, "Sir, no, sir." Looking away from me, Mr. Dye explained it was the knob who had sexually harassed me.

I felt my heart break, but I kept my face stony as I said, "Sir, yes, sir." For a moment, I couldn't breathe. Shifting uncomfortably, Mr. Dye asked me how I felt about him being chosen. Swallowing hard, I replied, "Sir, no excuse, sir." There was a long silence.

Mr. Dye looked at me again, his face sad, unable to express what he wanted to say. At last he said, "Mace, I don't know what I am trying to say, but . . . I mean, do you know what I am trying to say?"

I replied, "Sir, yes, sir."

After another moment of silence, Mr. Dye turned and left the room. Still bracing, I could see him leave out of the corner of my eye. He paused a moment by the door to look at me, a shadow in the doorway, and then closed the door gently behind him. The sunlight disappeared.

I continued to stand there, staring at the light switch on the wall, tears stinging my eyes. I was not on the Commandant's List. Yet, Mr. Dye, the harshest and toughest in my company, had just told me in his own awkward way that I deserved the honor. Pain and wonder struggled in my heart. Not knowing what else to do, I called my mother. Then, and only then, I cried.

I knew that the best revenge was success, so instead of giving up, I worked even harder to achieve. I also began to involve myself in the school's efforts to improve the Assimilation Plan for Women. The college was struggling to straighten out the mess surrounding the "M&M" disaster, and I was more than willing to help them do it. I wanted something positive to come out of the problems as much as the administration did, so I volunteered for every board and committee that met that semester on women's issues. I worked on everything from choosing women's uniforms, to educating cadets on sexual harassment, to creating procedures to deal with cadet menstrual periods. My participation gave me a sense of power, of control, that helped me get through the hard times in the battalion. I knew that every painful moment I suffered could be used to help the females that would follow me someday.

I even started to have fun now and then with the subject of being a woman in a man's world. One night for evening mess, I rewrote the "purpose of the cadet system" to fit my gender and popped it off during dinner as my Mess Fact. "Why can't women cadets wear heels to formation? Why can't women cadets wear makeup to muster? Why must we hold door for all 'gentlemen'?" On and on I went, and when I finished, my mess carver told me my performance was outstanding and sat me in the place of honor. Sometimes it is the little victories that keep you going.

Early in February, I was given an honor that helped make up for being left off the Commandant's List. I was awarded The Citadel Gold Stars, the highest award at the college for academic achievement—me, the girl who had almost flunked out of school a few years before. I was thrilled.

The awards ceremony itself was amazing. Gold Stars are handed out once every semester at Friday Parade. That Friday, instead of marching with my company as usual, I formed part of an honor company of about seventy Gold Star recipients. We marched together to the center of the field and stood at attention as General Poole explained to the audience that we were being recognized as the best cadets in the Corps academically. Then the general and three other officers walked down the lines as we stood in formation, to hand us our stars personally.

I could see Colonel Gordon making his way down my line out of the corner of my right eye. As he got close to me, a crowd of reporters rushed out with cameras and boom microphones to record the event. I pretended not to see them. When the colonel finally reached me, he removed a piece of blue velvet cardboard with two brass stars on it from a tray held by an accompanying cadet, then handed me the stars. With a warm smile, he shook my hand and congratulated me. I smiled back and replied, "Sir, thank you, sir," and saluted. My cheeks were burning. I knew my parents were watching from the stands. Then the colonel moved on to the next cadet, and I stood unmoving, my heart still pounding with excitement, as the rest of the stars were handed out.

Afterward, I met my parents near the stands, where they were already surrounded by waiting photographers. My mother gave me a big hug, and my father glowed, unable to conceal his excitement. The next day papers across the nation carried a picture of me beaming at a well-wisher on the edge of the Parade grounds, my father's right arm draped around my shoulder. My father's face in the photo glows with pride and affection. The look on my dad's face that day was better than the Gold Stars. I had finally made him proud of me. That alone made it all worthwhile.

A few days later, I received a packet of essays from seventh-graders I had coached in swimming, congratulating me on my achievement. One boy wrote, "Nancy was always a person I could look up to. I have no doubt that she will finish The Citadel with a smile on her face. I definitely think women should be allowed to go to The Citadel. Especially ones like Nancy Mace." I had become a role model. It felt wonderful.

By far the biggest surprise of the semester came two weeks later, in mid-February. The fall-out from the M&M investigation had been disastrous for the college, and every policy in the school, written and unwritten, was being examined. Along with the policy changes, major changes were occurring at the top level of administrators. A search for a new president was going on long before the legal problems started, and General Grinalds had already been chosen for that position. He was a good man, and I was pleased with the choice. The word in the Corps was that the school was also looking for a new commandant, the second in command next to The Citadel president. As the officer directly responsible for military training, Corps policy, and cadet discipline, the commandant was the most important administrator on campus in the eyes of the cadets. That position had not yet been filled.

One Friday at lunch mess, when announcements are traditionally made, the departing commandant, Colonel Trez, got up to speak. He began by explaining that he would be accepting another position at the College, and that a new commandant would be arriving next week to take over his duties. Colonel Trez then began going on and on about how much he loved the school, and how the new man loved the school even more. I really wasn't paying much attention as the colonel explained that the new man was a Citadel grad, but when he said that "this man" was a 1963 graduate and the former cadet commander of F-Troop, I stopped chewing and swallowed hard. "What?" The Colonel went on. "This outstanding officer served in the U.S. Army and commanded the first-ever Ranger Brigade." "Oh my gosh," I thought, as I quickly refilled my glass with red stuff and started drinking. "Served with the 82nd Airborne Division. The most decorated living graduate of The Citadel. A man who knew how to get the job done." Here it came. I refilled my glass once more and started to gulp. "Ladies and gentlemen, your new commandant will be Brigadier General Emory Mace."

Every head in the Mess Hall turned immediately toward my table, and I could feel hundreds of eyes fixed on me as a murmur ran around the room. I felt my face turn beet red, but I kept my head lowered and continued drinking. I didn't know what else to do. Finally, my mess carver said, "How long have you known about this, Mace?"

The cadet sitting to my right said, "Your dad is a real hard ass, isn't he, Mace?"

I murmured, "Sir, yes, sir," and crammed my hamburger in my mouth. He had no idea just how tough my father was. The man used to keep alligators in his room to scare knobs. Every cadet at the table was staring at me in shock. I had a sudden, overwhelming urge to giggle, so I just kept eating and drinking as fast as I could to hide my nervousness. After what seemed like forever, lunch ended, and I was dismissed.

I rushed straight back to my room, my mind racing. I knew General

Grinalds had come to my parents' house a few weeks before to talk to my dad about the position. My father had talked to me afterward, asking for my opinion. He said he had turned General Grinalds down, mostly out of concern for me, for he knew that being the commandant's daughter would make my life in the Corps an even bigger hell. If I was opposed, he told me, he wouldn't even consider it further. He even went so far as to turn down the offer a second time.

I knew he was right about the harassment I'd be in for, but I also knew that my father was desperately needed at the College. He had the experience, the judgment, and the common sense to fix what needed fixing. I told him that I knew it would be hard for me, but that if he wanted the job, I would support him. Besides, I told him, The Citadel needed him. There was so much that needed to be done there, and my father was perfect for the job.

That was the last I'd heard of the subject until the day at lunch mess. The minute I reached my quarters that afternoon, I grabbed the phone and called my father. No answer. I called him again after class, and this time he picked up the phone. "Good afternoon, Dad," I said.

"Good afternoon," he replied. "So, Nancy. How was lunch?" And he started to laugh.

I said, "Geez, Dad, thanks for telling me you accepted the job!" Then I went on to tell him what had happened during lunch. My dad was laughing so hard, I wondered if he could hear me. Finally, he calmed down, and we talked about it for a minute. I told him not to worry, that I was fine with his decision. He told me he'd be moving into his new office the next week, but for the time being, he and my mother would remain in Goose Creek. For the time being, he was only acting commandant. He and Mom wanted to see how everything worked out before he took the position on a permanent basis.

"Oh, and Nancy," he said as I got ready to sign off. "You do know that while I'm commandant of The Citadel, you're not my daughter. You're just another cadet."

"I know, Dad, I know." And I hung up. It was a sobering thought.

The remainder of the semester seemed to go by at light speed. My father moved into his office, and just as he'd promised, I was not his daughter while I was in uniform. He began a series of investigations and of changes that affected discipline on every level of the Corps. Upperclassmen would no longer be allowed to make their own rules, with no respect for College policy. The changes did not make my father very popular, and they made my life hell second semester. Now I was not only the "bitch," but the "son-of-a-bitch's kid." My father might not recognize our relationship on campus, but every cadet in the Corps sure did, and they made me pay for it. Like every other knob on campus, I hung in and dreamed of May and Recognition Day.

CHAPTER 15

RECOGNITION DAY

Recognition Day is the official end to the Fourth Class System. It comes the third week in May, a few days before graduation. On that day, freshman are "recognized" as equals by upperclassmen, which means knobs can now call cadets of every level by their first names instead of "Mr. So-and-So." Recognition also brings an end to the nonstop racking, bracing, and dirty work of freshman year. The catch is that Recognition Day is also the cadre's last chance to harass their knobs, and they take full advantage of the privilege.

Knob year begins in September with Hell Night. It ends nine months later in purgatory. The difference between hell and purgatory is that if you survive purgatory, you get to go to a better place. Recognition Day was my purgatory.

On that hot, muggy morning in spring, I was awakened at 0500 by the sound of rhythmic clapping, pounding on my door, and shouts of "Wake up, knobs! Wake up!" It was Hell Week all over again. I threw on my summer PTs and was out on the quad with my company ten minutes later, marking time with my broom for the first of many Sweep Details that day. The upperclassmen racked us at the top of their lungs as we lifted our knees broom high. Within five minutes, my face was covered with sweat and the spit that flew from the cadre's mouths as they screamed at us.

Shortly after 0530, we were marched out the front sally port to the Parade Field, where a small group of press photographers waited. The flash of their cameras was the only light in the dark field. On order, I dropped with the other knobs and began a series of nonstop exercises: push-ups, sit-ups, scissor kicks, and squat thrusts. As I lay on my back to do curls, I was dimly aware that the stars were still out in the charcoal gray sky overhead. They blurred through the sweat running in my eyes.

For more than an hour, I curled, pushed, squatted, and lifted until every muscle in my body burned like fire. Just when I knew I couldn't do one more push-up, the platoon sergeant ordered us to stand up. Staggering to my feet, I heard the next command: "Run, knobbies, run!" And off we went, around the Parade Field, then all the way around campus, as my legs slowly turned to jelly. By the time we made it back to the Parade Field, the sun was just peeking over the horizon. "One more hour!" an upperclassman shouted. I choked back a groan. I didn't think I could get through another minute.

Down the field from me, I could see Echo Company doing a "firefighters' drill." Each knob had to pick up a classmate, throw him over his shoulder, and carry him twenty yards down the field to where an upperclassman waited. I saw Petra heave a fellow knob over her shoulder and start gamely toward her officer. If she could do this, so could I. I felt a surge of determination flow back into my exhausted body.

Meanwhile, the Band Company commander had ordered us into a drill called the "circle of death." We formed a large circle on the grass, lying on our stomachs, hands and feet in position for push-ups. Then on order, we pushed ourselves off the ground and arched our backs like cats, creating a human tunnel. One at a time, our classmates had to crawl the full length of the tunnel, then take their positions again as part of the arch. One of my classmates slipped and fell as he crawled on the grass, still slick with dew. "Get up, knobbie! You can do this! Think about all you've been through!" shouted the sergeant. The knob struggled back onto his knees and continued crawling. A few yards away I could hear the rhythm of jogging feet and the rhythmic chanting, "We are! Echo!" as Echo Company jogged by, clapping. Our circle completed, we pulled ourselves to our feet and jogged after them.

I don't know how long the running and the drilling went on. It felt like forever. The sun came up, lighting the white walls that rose all around us, and still we kept running. The moisture on the Parade Field had dried long before we were ordered back to the barracks for more drilling and Sweep Details. I vaguely remember being marched over to the Mess Hall at some point for breakfast mess and more racking. I was too tired to eat. It was all I could do to brace my body on the edge of the chair while I thirstily drank down glass after glass of water. Then more marching, a quick trip to the latrine, and it all started again.

Hours passed in a blur. A short break, a drink of water, and we'd be off and running again. Finally, nearly three hours after we'd been roused abruptly from sleep, Cadet Colonel Butler ordered all the companies back to the battalions for our final round of push-ups. Inside the barracks we formed circles by company, Band Company making the center circle in the red and white quad. Each upperclassman chose a knob and kneeled down next to him, to count push-ups and help him finish if he couldn't make it alone. Mr. Wizeman chose me. The number of required push-ups on Recognition Day changed each year. The year before, the class of 1999 had to do 99 push-ups. My class, the class of 2000, had to do 100.

By then my arms were so weak, they felt like dead weights on my shoulders. I wasn't about to give up, but I wasn't sure my body would do what I told it to. As I dragged myself into position, Mr. Wizeman kneeled down and very quietly placed a small object on the tile in front of me. I hadn't heard anything about this being part of the tradition. I blinked in bewilderment and looked closer. It was a tiny silver cross, the sort you wear around your neck. I looked up at Mr. Wizeman. His face was serious as he told me to place my hands squarely on top of the cross. Neither of us said a word about the small piece of silver lying on the tile beneath me, but as my fingers touched the metal, Mr. Wizeman's message came through loud and clear. I began to lift my body off the ground, up and down, one painful shove at a time.

By the time I reached my thirtieth push-up, my arms simply refused to lift me one more time. When that happened, Mr. Wizeman pulled a towel under my stomach, gripped the ends, and stood over me. Then he pulled me upward, like an injured animal in a sling, and continued counting: "Thirty-one, thirty-two. . . ." I did my best to help, shoving my back toward him. My muscles were collapsing, but my mind was still strong. All around me, my classmates were being helped in the same way. Some upperclassmen used towels; others grabbed the backs of the knobs' shirts and pulled upward. One way or another, we would not be allowed to fail. In a haze of exhaustion, I finally heard Mr. Wizeman's voice call out, "One hundred." My body collapsed on the ground like a dead thing. I had done it. We had done it.

There was only one more obstacle to go. A few yards away, in the center of our circle of struggling knobs, our company commander stood holding the Band Company guidon. He held the long pole upright, its base pressed down against the tile, the banner fluttering overhead. As each of us finished our last push-up, we were ordered to remain on the ground and crawl over to the company guidon. Once there, we were told to grab the pole and lie there, holding on. Clutching the small silver cross in my hand, I began to crawl toward the guidon on Mr. Wizeman's order. Soaked in sweat, my bare knees and hands slid on the slippery surface as I struggled across the endless yards of red and white tiles to join my class. Once there, I had to pull myself over the top of a classmate's body to grab onto the pole. Limp with exhaustion, I held on as one by one, every knob in my company made his painful way across the quad to our guidon.

I heard a groan escape me as another knob pulled himself onto my back to reach the pole. We lay there in a heap, like a pile of dead fish, unable to move. By the time the last of my classmates reached the banner, we had formed a pile of dark, sweaty, stinking bodies several feet high. It was hard to breathe. Someone ordered us to close our eyes. Then, on command, we began to pop off the Cadet Prayer in unison for the last time as knobs. I was surprised at the strength of my own voice as I settled into the rhythm of the chanting. All around me, my classmates' voices also got stronger as we recited the prayer together that one last time. As we sounded off, our eyes still closed in the musky darkness of that human mound, the upperclassmen circled us in silence. Every now and then, one would bend down to touch us with a pat or a tap on the shoulder as a way of saying, "Good job, knob." I felt one, two, three pats on the back. Joy and relief began to wash through me. Tears mixed with the perspiration on my face as we pledged to "endure hardship" for a worthy cause. I had endured. We all had.

When the prayer ended, we heard Cadet Colonel Butler's voice over the PA system once again, ordering us to rise and line up by company. I made my way slowly over to the letters on the far side of the quad, to line up with my classmates. Mike McKee and I took our places at the head of the line, in the place of honor reserved for the clerks—the best two knobs in the company. Our company commander carried the Band guidon to the head of our line and handed it to Mike and me. We held it carefully between us, our hands tightly gripping the pole, and then braced one last time with the rest of our classmates. As we came to attention, Mr. Butler ordered us to close our eyes. Very quietly, the upperclassmen in each of the five companies lined up behind their commanders and waited. The whole scene was eerily reminiscent of Hell Night nine months earlier. In every battalion on campus, I knew, the same scene was taking place.

Quiet settled over the battalions one by one, until the entire campus lay hushed and waiting. The afternoon sun blazed overhead, the heavy Charleston air pressing down on our bodies in the silence. Out of the corner of my eye, I could see my father's stocky figure near the front sally port, chewing his cigar and watching the remarkable change that was about to take place. Nerves strained to their limit, my body began to tremble with exhaustion and excitement.

Finally, the public address system crackled to life, and I heard Mr. Butler's voice through the speakers, as solemn and commanding as it had been on Hell Night. He began to speak to us, and as he did, I heard the distant notes of a bagpipe playing "Home, Sweet Home" in the background. My mind shot back to that terrifying Wednesday night nine months before, when I had stood in the darkness with strangers, wondering what lay ahead of me. Now those strangers were my brothers.

As the bagpipes continued to play, every knob in the battalion was overwhelmed with emotion. I felt tears well up in my eyes. Mike's hand trembled next to mine on the guidon, and the emotion we held back was like an electric current running through my body and down the line to my classmates. Mr. Butler's voice continued, telling us what we already knew: that our days as knobs had ended, and that we were now being welcomed as full-fledged members of The South Carolina Corps of Cadets. Petra and I were about to become what no other women had ever been: upperclassmen. At last, as the bagpipes began to fade, I heard Commander Butler's voice telling us to quit bracing. My chin came forward and my spine relaxed as I settled into a normal posture. And finally, the words I had struggled for nine months to hear were spoken quietly in Mr. Butler's soft Southern drawl: "Cadets, the Fourth Class System is no longer in effect." The bagpipes fell silent. I had to hold onto the guidon pole with all my strength in the exhilaration of that moment.

And then, like a receiving line in reverse, the upperclassmen from my company began to come down the freshman line. Assembled according to class, with the seniors first, every cadet in Band Company introduced himself by his first name, shook my hand, and congratulated me. I cannot describe the intensity of those moments as the same men who had harassed me for nine months shook my hand and welcomed me as an equal. Tears hovered just behind my lower lashes, but I did not let them spill over. Halfway through the line of upperclassmen, I looked up to see Mr. Wizeman's kind face in front of me. Saying simply, "Nancy, I'm Scott. Welcome to the company," he reached out and took my hand. I gripped his with all my strength and shook it. He looked at me a moment, then moved on. I bit my lip, then turned to the next cadet. Wedged tightly between the fingers that held the guidon was my small silver cross.

Only when the last hand in all four battalions had been shaken were we all dismissed. As Mr. Butler's voice gave the order for dismissal, insanity broke loose. Every freshman in the place, newly released from nine months of prison, went crazy. We screamed and yelled and ran around and pounded each other on the back, suddenly filled with energy. In keeping with long tradition, each platoon grabbed the highest-ranking company cadet officer in sight and carried him off to the showers for a cold soaking. The captured cadets yelled and struggled in protest, but none of them really tried to get away. Doubled up laughing, I looked up just in time to see that my platoon had snagged the biggest fish of all. My mouth gaped open as I watched my classmates carry my father, cigar still clenched in his teeth, off to the female showers. They soaked him to the skin in his uniform and hat while I watched, my own uniform clinging damply to my body.

Joy washed over me like a baptism. My new life was just beginning.

EPILOGUE:
WEARING THE RING

Two years and several lifetimes later, I sat among rows of cadets in McAllister Fieldhouse and waited to hear my name called. My white skirt was sharply pressed for the last time, my gold stars carefully arrayed on my collar. My hair had grown out, curling gently behind my ears, still short by civilian standards. I wore pale lipstick, clear nail polish, and mascara—all within the new standards for upperclass female cadets. On my right hand, outlined beneath my white cotton glove, was a heavy gold Citadel ring.

Much had changed at The Citadel since I had walked into the Padgett–Thomas Barracks three years earlier. Two dozen women had entered the previous fall, and more were applying every day. Women now held rank in every class. I had been a part of that change every step of the way, drafting letters for the College recruiters to mail, making countless public speaking appearances on behalf of the school, serving on innumerable committees. The uniform I was wearing had changed as well; Petra and I had served as mannequins for a whole series of experimental uniforms for female cadets. The traditional gray trousers remained the same for duty uniforms and drill, but women could now go on leave or attend special functions dressed in skirts. I was satisfied with the women's uniforms, as I was with the new haircut requirements for upperclass female cadets. Shoes and covers now came in women's sizes, and the gift shop carried pantyhose and five different kinds of tampons. Women no longer felt like strangers in their own college.

My father's term as commandant had also brought about sweeping reforms, changes that had angered many of the cadets. Discipline had become lax and inconsistent during the ten years before I entered the Corps. When I'd arrived as a freshman, the upperclass had a free hand in disciplining the knobs, but showed a lack of discipline themselves. Too often the unwritten rule had been "Do as I say, not as I do," with upperclassmen forcing standards on freshmen that they themselves couldn't meet. Upperclass cadets were not required to do physical training my freshman year, not required to follow most of the rules they'd imposed on me, not required to report to administrators. The cadre ran the cadre, with little interference from anyone. Most of the cadet officers in Band Company were honorable people who had behaved responsibly, but a few abused their position and took advantage of those they outranked. My father had put an end to those abuses.

He'd also made the cadre practice what they preached. Dad had revived the old tradition of making knobs drop and do push-ups. Using push-ups as punishment had been against the rules when I was a freshman. Plenty of cadet officers made us do it, but usually behind closed doors where the administrators wouldn't find out about it. My father made the practice "legal" again. Cadets could now make knobs drop and do push-ups whenever they wanted, with the school's blessing. There was only one catch: The cadre had to drop with their knobs and match them, push-up for push-up, and still have enough breath to rack while they did. The new rule forced the cadre to stay in shape, and to dish out only what they could chew. When I became cadet sergeant the second semester of my sophomore year, I ordered my own knobs to drop, but I dropped with them. It encouraged mutual respect.

Physical training was once again required for all cadets, with everyone expected to meet the minimum standards. No more chunky cadre yelling at freshman to do calisthenics. Cadet officers now ran with them. Supervision and accountability had improved all the way up the line, from the greenest knob to the commandant. Things would always happen outside the rules every now and then, but not much had gotten past my dad. Every cadet in the Corps knew the stories of my father's alligator-poaching days, and they had no desire to mess with him. They called him "Bulldog," often growling when he walked by. My dad really was the toughest son-of-a-bitch on campus, and everyone knew it. The Corps' fear of him was matched only by their respect.

When I finished freshman year, I'd thought things would get easier for me. I had been dead wrong. Knobs are harassed, but they are also protected by the cadet officers responsible for them. Once I became a sophomore, there was no one to watch out for me, and I became the target of increased abuse. Making the situation even worse, I became involved in a serious romantic relationship with one of the highest ranking cadets in the Corps. The relationship itself was miserable and unhealthy, the result of my loneliness and sense of isolation on campus, but when I tried to break it off, I found he wouldn't let me. Against my strong protests, my boyfriend resigned his position to be with me, eventually destroying my personal property and leaving disturbing notes in my quarters when I refused to go out with him anymore. While struggling to free myself from him, I went from being "the bitch" to being "the whore" in the eyes of the Corps, the target of vicious remarks from cadets and alumni both. I was the slut who had ruined a promising young career. It was a nightmare. I swore never to make the same mistake, and it wasn't until senior year that I became romantically involved with a friend of mine, another cadet named Chris Niemiec. When Scott Wizeman graduated at the end of my second year, I felt more alone than ever.

Most people assumed that my father's position with the College during my last two years gave me an inside track, but the opposite was true. It only made life harder for me. My dad went as far as possible in the other direction when it came to favoritism. He did not speak to me on campus, and I was only allowed to come to his office on official business, which was seldom. The one time I dropped by unannounced, he flew out of his chair with a roar and kicked me out. I understood why he did it, but it stung. The hardest part, though, was that I was no longer just hazed for being a girl, but also for being my father's daughter. When I walked alone behind the battalions, the galleries would often echo with anonymous voices shouting, "Why don't you and your shitbag father get the fuck out of our school!" I would raise my chin and walk straight ahead, but the comments hurt and infuriated me, as much for my father as for myself.

I'd become hardened to the criticism after a while. I had to get tough to survive. There had been some things, though, that I'd never gotten used to. The vicious, personal nature of the gossip still hurt. I had been accused of everything imaginable, from being a drunk to being a drug addict. When I spent time with Petra or mentored female knobs, the whisper went around that I was a "dyke." If I so much as looked at a male cadet, I was a slut. According to campus gossip, I'd had several abortions and more than one illegitimate child. I had been called ugly, stupid, bitch, whore, and worse, more times than I could count. Those who knew me realized that the rumors weren't true, and that the names were cruel and unjust, but still, it bothered me that people I would never meet still smeared my reputation far and wide. It was humiliating, and it was unfair. I sometimes felt like I'd had a stomachache for three years, just from holding in my feelings.

Even the Ring Ceremony, usually the pinnacle of a cadet's time at The Citadel, had been a struggle for me. As I sat in the fieldhouse that warm graduation morning, my fingers curled reflexively over the gold band on my right ring finger. My mind drifted back seven months, to the day I first slid it on.

I had wanted that Citadel ring desperately from the first day I walked through Lesegne Gate. Wearing the same ring my dad wore would be the tangible proof that I really was my father's daughter. From my earliest memories, I could picture my father's hand wearing that amazing circle of gold. It is an unusually large ring, solid gold, bearing the seal of the Corps, with carving all around. I knew my father had literally been willing to lose his life for it, and I had always known that, along with his Bible, The Citadel ring was my father's most treasured possession.

Getting my own ring had not only required surviving life in the Corps, as the male cadets had to do; it also meant a prolonged battle with the administration and Board of Visitors. The Citadel old guard wanted to give senior female cadets miniature rings, tiny replicas of the male ring identical to those given as love tokens by male cadets to their girlfriends. After three years in the Corps, I had no intention of accepting a ring most women got just for being a good date! I fought for, and eventually got, a female ring that was an 85 percent replica of the male ring—slightly smaller and less heavy than the male version, but otherwise identical in every way.

The problem didn't even end there, though. When my ring was finally ordered, I discovered that my ring form had been tampered with. Someone had pulled my paperwork from the file and published the words of the personal inscription I had ordered for the inside of the band. Furious, I changed the inscription, keeping the new one under lock and key until the rings actually arrived. But the final insult came when the cadets receiving their rings with me protested my presence at the Ring Ceremony. I had entered The Citadel as a member of the Class of 2000, but because of my transfer credits from a previous college, I would be graduating with the Class of 1999. The Class of '99 had spent the last three years bragging that they were the "last all-male graduating class," and they did not want me graduating with them, did not want me wearing a ring with a '99 on it. I knew I would get my ring only over their loud objections.

By the time Ring Ceremony rehearsal came around, in October of my senior year, I was a nervous wreck. Rumors had been floating around campus for weeks that the Corps would boo me during the next day's ceremony. The tension at the rehearsal was definite, and everyone could feel the hostility in the air. Sitting among the other seniors in the chapel that afternoon, I had to force my attention back to the podium as my father stepped up to speak. As commandant, it was his job to speak to the senior cadets about the significance of The Citadel ring. I had no idea what he was going to say, but as he eyed the crowd and began to speak, I recognized the opening words of a story I had heard since childhood. He was telling the seniors about the day he rescued *his* ring.

The story he told that day was about a mission in Vietnam. My father was stationed there during the Vietnam War, as part of a three-man advisory team to a South Vietnamese battalion of paratroopers. The team was made up of a captain, a lieutenant, and a senior sergeant. My dad was the lieutenant and wasn't much over twenty-five years old at the time. One afternoon he was with a company of one hundred of the paratroopers, in some rice paddies outside a small village, when they became engaged in a fierce battle with a large North Vietnamese force about 100 yards away. For four hours, he lay in a foot of water behind a rice paddy dike, bullets hitting all around him. After ten months of combat, he had lost over fifty pounds, and both his wedding ring and his college ring had gotten loose. Sometime shortly before nightfall, he felt his Citadel ring slip off and sink into the marshy water below him. With bullets hitting the water, he didn't dare go in after his ring. When night fell, his unit fell back about a mile to friendly forces under the cover the darkness. He knew his ring was close to the enemy's location, but he had no intention of leaving it there. He asked his captain for permission to return and retrieve the ring. The captain was a VMI man himself, and he understood the importance of my father's ring, so he gave my father permission to return. My dad refused to take anyone with him, as he wasn't willing to risk any life but his own.

My father felt at home in the marshes at night, just as he had been in the swamps of South Carolina as a boy, but what he was about to attempt was incredibly dangerous. The enemy was still hidden among the trees and the tall bushes, and it was impossible to see them in the pitch blackness of the Vietnam countryside. My father had only his instinct to guide him, but knew he could find the exact spot where he'd lain in the water for all those hours—and his ring. No one in his right mind would have attempted such a mission. No one, that is, except my father.

It took him nearly two hours to make his way stealthily through the rice paddy, carefully retracing his path of the evening before. While moving quietly down the trails on the rice paddy dike, he encountered two North Vietnamese soldiers and killed them with his rifle. Finally managing to reach the spot where he had lain, he lay down and began to search. In the blackness of the moonless night, my dad searched the water, groping blindly through the silt for the familiar shape, his senses constantly alert for the approach of enemy soldiers. Finally, after searching for quite some time, he stumbled onto what he knew was his ring. Grasping the prize tightly, he slid the muddy ring onto the third finger of his right hand. Then, as silently as the alligators he had once trapped, he made his way back to camp. He encountered one more North Vietnamese soldier on his way back, shooting this one as well. Just as the sun began to rise, my father emerged from the darkness, the ring of The South Carolina Corps of Cadets once more on his hand. It has remained there ever since.

Listening to my father's matter-of-fact voice telling the familiar story, I raised my eyes to his face. For once, he had removed his cigar for this ceremonial occasion. Two years earlier, I had come to this place to make this man, my childhood hero, proud. At the time, he had doubted I could do it. I had endured every form of abuse to prove to him, and to myself, that I could. I straightened my spine. If my father could battle Viet Cong to claim his ring, I could certainly face a few dozen sexist cadets to claim mine.

By the next morning, friends and families of the cadets, along with members of the press, were arriving by the hundreds. Rings are given on Parents' Weekend each year, and every corner of the campus was crowded with visitors that day. Seniors traditionally invite their families and a special date to participate in the Ring Ceremony with them. I didn't have a serious boyfriend, and my brother James was already a freshman at West Point, so he couldn't escort me. I really needed a friend, and in characteristic fashion, my old mentor came to the rescue. Scott Wizeman had graduated the spring before and gotten married a month after. I had been an acolyte in his wedding. He and his wife were living in Dallas, where Scott was attending seminary to prepare for a career as an Army chaplain. We had continued to write and e-mail after they left South Carolina, so that October Scott flew all the way from Dallas, with his wife's blessing, to be my "date" for Ring Week. I was so glad to see him that I nearly cried. Although he didn't say so, I knew he was there for moral support, and he knew what my ring meant to me. He also knew what might happen when I received it.

It is impossible to explain the importance of the Ring Ceremony to someone outside the Corps. In some respects, the ceremony is more important than graduation. Rings are awarded in Summerall Chapel. Only family members are allowed inside the sanctuary, which is always packed to the walls. On that fall afternoon, I took my place with the other seniors in my company inside the walls of 2nd Battalion, the Band Company Barracks. Because the battalion is located next to the Parade Field, directly across from the chapel, all the companies had been ordered to assemble there. The tiled quad was filled that day with cadets in dress uniform lined up by battalion and company, in alphabetical order. We formed two long columns, lined up side by side. As I moved to take my place, several cadets followed me with their eyes, their faces filled with angry resentment. I stepped into line with Band Company, right in front of Mr. Mitchell, my old nemesis from knob year. We had ended up graduating together. He gave me a brief nod of encouragement. I lifted my chin and put on my brave face, looking, I hoped, every inch the soldier. My stomach began to ache. Surely the senior class wouldn't disgrace me, or the Corps, by hissing in the chapel sanctuary. I could feel the sweat break out on my upper lip.

A lone drummer took his place in the center of the Parade Field. Silence fell over the campus. Then with a sharp report, the drummer began to strike cadence. In perfect sequence, we began to march steadily forward, across the Parade Field and up the steps into Summerall Chapel. As I followed my classmates from Band Company onto the field, I was aware of reporters straining to take my photograph. Eyes straight ahead, I marched across the field and into the chapel, straight down the center aisle to our assigned pew. I caught a glimpse of my parents in the back row. The building was packed. On order, we all sat down.

A series of administrators and guests got up to speak to the crowd of families and cadets. After fifteen minutes of greetings and preliminaries, officials took their places for the conferring of the rings. I saw photographers move quietly to the side of the podium and focus their cameras on the altar. A table was covered with a white cloth, and in place of the cross and the articles of the sacrament was row upon row of small blue boxes. As President Grinalds stepped forward to begin the proceedings, a wave of nausea swept over me, and I began to sweat, as I had no idea what would happen when my name was called.

Officials began to call us up, row by row, to receive a handshake and the small velvet boxes containing the prized memento. As each cadet came forward, he was given a congratulatory handshake and presented with an open box containing his ring. Each battalion had elected one of its own tactical officers for the actual presentation. Colonel Dorton, the barracks officer, would be handing me my ring. Standing in line in the side aisle, I waited my turn as the colonel called out the names of seniors in my battalion. At last I heard him call, "Nancy Ruth Mace."

Taking a deep breath and ignoring the pain in my stomach, I stepped forward to the front of the altar. As I did, loud hissing began to fill the air. The beautiful sanctuary, lovely in the afternoon sun, suddenly sounded like a roomful of angry snakes. The cadets themselves glared at me silently, having been ordered by their superior officers to maintain discipline. But their families were under no such order. Their venom filled the air. The hissing from the back of the church reached a crescendo as I shook Colonel Dorton's hand and took the velvet box. My stomach shuddered uncontrollably, but I smiled bravely into the camera as the colonel congratulated me. Then, putting on my stone face once again, I held back the tears that burned behind my eyeballs and walked quietly down the center aisle to my seat. In the back of the sanctuary, I could see my mother's face, pale with anger and worry. Even my father, with a face as stoical as the "Bulldog" he's nicknamed for, was visibly upset. He glared at the senior cadets assembled in front of him. I wondered briefly if they could feel the heat of his eyes on the backs of their heads.

When the last senior had received his ring and made his way back down the aisle, the Chaplain rose and asked the congregation to join him in the Prayer of The Citadel. Standing there next to my classmates, still clutching the box containing my ring, I added my small voice to the deep male voices all around me. When the prayer ended, General Grinalds rose and solemnly announced, "Class of '99, you may now put on your rings."

I looked wonderingly down at the box and the burnished gold ring inside. It was exactly like my father's, except for the battle scars his still wore. Well, I had a few battle scars of my own. Mine, though, were on my heart. As I slipped the ring onto my trembling finger, a mixture of pain and joy washed over me, and I had to fight back tears. Everything except the ring blurred around me. A few minutes later, we filed back outside and onto the Avenue of Remembrance, where Scott and my parents waited in a crowd of reporters. I rushed into my parents' embrace.

Laughing and crying, surrounded by media, I showed my ring to my father. One of the photographers asked my dad to show them his ring, too. Dad was happy to oblige. The following day the papers were filled with photographs of the two rings, my small hand on my father's. It was one of the proudest moments of my life.

As dusk began to descend, our little party separated, as I would not be celebrating like the other seniors. I knew there was a special meal planned for seniors in the Mess Hall in a few minutes, but I also knew I wouldn't be welcome there. Still, I was determined not to be scared away, so I gave my parents a last hug and told them I'd meet them for dinner in an hour. The pain in my stomach had finally gone away. Racing back to the battalion to change into my uniform skirt and blazer, I was astonished to see two rows of my classmates—nearly all of whom wouldn't graduate until the next year—forming a path across the checkered quad. They were doing push-ups and sounding off in unison. It was the cadet way of honoring seniors, of showing us respect. They knew what had happened to me a short while earlier in the chapel. This was their way of telling me that whatever the other cadets thought, they were still my brothers. My cheeks glowed as I made my way between the rows of my classmates, and walked across the quad into my own room.

Evan Reich, who was also graduating early, waited for me to change, and together we rushed over to the Mess Hall to join the other Band Company seniors. As we entered, the hissing began again, and followed us as we made our way to our table. I knew that the company seniors would be going out drinking together after the meal, for that was another Citadel tradition. I had stuck to my resolve not to drink with other cadets, but I was hoping they might ask me to join them as a designated driver, so that I wouldn't have to miss out completely. They did not. In fact, Mr. Sharp made it quite clear that they did not want me with them. He wasn't about to have a female who had once been his knob sharing his ring celebration with him. I stared down at my plate as the others laughed and joked, chewing on the stringy steak that had been served to them. Once more, I struggled to hold back tears. I hadn't really expected to be invited, but I'd thought that just maybe. . . . Reich and

Mitchell sat quietly next to me. Every now and then, Evan would whisper something encouraging. Evan wasn't invited, either, for he was also graduating ahead of his class. I knew they both felt terrible. Containing the tears that threatened to spill over my lashes, I told them I would be fine, then I headed back across campus to join my family.

We had a wonderful evening together. My parents and Scott took me to Carolinas on Exchange Street, one of the finest seafood restaurants in Charleston, and one of the most elegant. Dad and Scott looked handsome in their suits, and we all ate and laughed and told stories—and everyone admired my ring. By the end of the meal, the pain in my chest had gone away, and I was feeling relaxed. Afterward, my parents drove back to campus and Scott and I walked around for hours on Market Street, talking and relishing our time together. We stopped by our favorite shop for steamed milk as we had in the old days, when we were usually the only two cadets who weren't drinking. The night was warm, and we heard the clop-clop of horses' hooves as we walked through downtown Charleston. By the time Scott took me back to the hushed campus, a deep peace had settled over me. Scott hugged me good-bye, and later when I crawled into bed, I slept like a baby.

I awoke renewed on Friday morning and enjoyed the weekly Parade, where there was a large turnout, the field filled with families there to see their children. The Ring Hop, the annual dance for seniors and their dates, was being held that night in McAllister Fieldhouse. As evening approached, I could feel the familiar dread beginning to knot up in my stomach again. Rumors were flying around campus that after restraining themselves in the chapel, the seniors planned to humiliate me at the hop. My parents had to leave early that evening to take their places in the reception line, so Scott helped me knot the burgundy sash on my full dress uniform and gave me a hasty inspection before we started the walk to the gym. A final mirror check showed my eyes dark against an unnaturally white face. We walked out into the musky air, still pleasantly warm even in October, and started down the road that led to the field-house. All around us, cadets and their dates were making the same journey. The only difference was, my "date" was a man.

As we stood in line at the entrance to the gym, I chatted nervously to Scott about everything except what waited for us inside. Gradually we made our way down the formal receiving line, shaking hands with General and Mrs. Grinalds, the vice president of Academic Affairs, and finally, my parents. All along the line, administrators asked to see my ring—the first of its kind—and afterward, Scott and I mingled with the other guests and waited for the big event of the evening.

A longstanding tradition at The Citadel honors seniors by having them "pass through the ring." The ring in this case is a giant replica, mounted on a platform in the middle of the fieldhouse. Company by company, each senior passes through the ring on the arm of his chosen companion. Again by tradition, the companion is the cadet's mother. Once through the ring, the cadet and his mother pass beneath an avenue of arched swords, raised in the cadet's honor. Their passage is usually greeted with warm applause and shouts of approval from the senior's buddies. The rumor was that on that night, the entire contingent of swordsmen would turn their backs to me as I emerged from the ring and started down the aisle of swords.

The wait for the grand moment felt endless. I was so nervous that I was having trouble keeping my composure. They finally called Band

Company, and I took my place in line. Choosing the companion who would share this honor with me had been easy. My father would accompany me through the ring—the first time in Citadel history that this had happened. I fingered the golden ring on my right hand nervously as the line inched forward. My father said little, and I too fell silent as we approached the symbolic ring arching ahead. When our turn came at last, I took my father's arm, and we ducked through the ring to the cheers of my mother and a few scattered friends. The avenue of arched swords was directly ahead, and as we approached the first pair of swordsmen, I prayed silently that they wouldn't turn their backs on us. I would survive the rude gesture, as I had so many others, but I couldn't bear the thought that they would show my father such disrespect. To my relief, the swordsmen remained rigidly in position, but as we passed under the first pair of swords, hissing broke out from other cadets in the room. I could feel the hostility radiating from the swordsmen. Holding my father's arm even tighter, I put on the stone face that had seen me through three long years. They might cause me pain, but I would never give them the satisfaction of letting them see it.

The ordeal finally ended and all I wanted to do was relax and talk to Scott. He taught me how to do a slow Shag, and as we danced and laughed, I began to feel better. At last I was too exhausted to dance another minute and although it was still early, I told Scott I wanted to go home. Physically and emotionally drained, we walked home in silence.

That had been seven months ago. Mr. Wizeman, my "guardian angel" of freshman year, had remained my faithful supporter until the end. Three years earlier, on Hell Night, he had made me promise that he would see me graduate one day. We had both kept that promise. He had been there to watch me receive my ring, and when my mother invited him and his wife to stay at my parents' house for my graduation, he never hesitated. I knew he was sitting a few yards away with his wife and my family in the fieldhouse on that warm May afternoon, having flown all the way from Texas to see me receive my diploma. The Citadel Code says that cadets keep their word. Scott was an honorable cadet. So was I.

So were many of the Corps. In spite of the prejudice of the hard-liners, I had formed friendships among the cadets that I would cherish for a lifetime. No one makes it alone at The Citadel, and my survival was a tribute to the Corps and the administration, not just to me. Like all graduates from that remarkable institution, I had formed lasting relationships with my classmates. Reich and Brooks, my old "Odd Squad" classmates from knob year, remained my buddies, bonded in a brotherhood of survival with roots that ran deep. Brooks had recently told a Charleston reporter that my graduation was an honor to all cadets. Alex Sparra was still my best pal, his mother an ongoing support to mine. Most of the cadets I'd worked with the last three years respected me, and many even liked me. Each semester, several more approached me to apologize for their attitude and tell me that they had learned to respect my contributions to the Corps. I'd also gotten poems and love letters from many cadets. Some were sweet and some were funny, but all were appreciated more than anyone will ever know. Without the support of these friends, I knew I would never be sitting with two hundred other graduating cadets, wearing the first senior ring ever given to a woman by The Citadel. For all the pain and bigotry I had suffered, I would not have traded that ring, or my three years in the Corps, for anything in the world.

And I had not only survived. I had distinguished myself. I knew I would be pointed to as the role model for every woman that followed me, and I took that responsibility very seriously. The achievements listed on my graduation announcement reflected how hard I'd worked. I'd been the first female to achieve cadet officer status, serving as company clerk, cadet sergeant, company executive officer, and finally academic officer for Band Company over a period of two and a half years. I had served on countless committees, helping create the policies that would affect Citadel women for generations to come. In spite of my ADD, I was graduating with a 3.74 GPA, and I was doing it in only three years. I had been on the President's List, Commandant's List, and the Dean's List. The school had awarded me Gold Stars every semester but one, and I had won awards from *The Wall Street Journal* and Beta Gamma Sigma. As a representative of the school, I had shaken the hands of generals and presidents, and my scrapbook was filled with letters from judges, governors, and even Gloria Steinem, the founding editor of *Ms.* magazine. I was extremely proud of what I had achieved and especially of what I represented—I was a Citadel woman. For three years, I had been sustained by the kindness of strangers, hundreds of well-wishers who'd sent me letters and e-mails of encouragement to get me through the tough times, and I knew I hadn't let them down.

It had been a fight to the very end. During the last few weeks Citadel administrators, fearing a fanatic might try to stop me from graduating, had shown me how to recognize a letter bomb and urged me to be especially watchful. So did my mother. She didn't tell me until afterward, but her anonymous correspondent, who still sent her hate mail, had hinted that something might happen to me at graduation. I thought their fears were groundless, but I was careful anyway. The years had not taught me fear, but they had taught me caution. I knew how to take care of myself.

I had proven myself in a man's world, and I had done it without giving up my womanhood. I smiled as I crooked the ring finger of my left hand. The fabric of my cotton glove caught for a moment on the sharp object beneath. After a year of friendship, I had begun dating fellow cadet Chris Niemiec a few weeks after the Ring Ceremony. Chris was a wonderful man who embodied the very best of the Corps. The night before, on the shore a few miles from the Beach House where I'd once celebrated the end of Hell Week, Chris had proposed. My left ring finger still tingled beneath the unaccustomed weight of the diamond engagement ring. As the honored guest on the podium droned on, I had to fight the urge to peel off my glove and gaze at the beauty of the sparkling stone beneath. It all seemed unreal, like an unexpectedly happy climax to a long movie. I hadn't come to The Citadel to find a man, but I was deeply grateful that such a fine one had found me.

Dragging my attention back to the dignitaries onstage in front of me, I realized that the keynote speaker for our graduating class was finally winding to a close. When at last he finished, General Grinalds stepped to the microphone and I sat up straighter in my seat. My heart began to race as he introduced The South Carolina Corps of Cadets Class of 1999. The general formally presented us to the audience amid shouts and cheers and I knew this was it. My final moment as a cadet. While the officials took their positions onstage, we were instructed to rise and make our way under the bleachers and around the back to the platform steps, where we would ascend and receive our diplomas.

As I filed quietly under the bleachers with the other cadets, my mind was racing. Every second of my life for three years had been spent striving for this moment, yet now that it was here, I was filled with panic. For the first time, it hit me: I was graduating. I was leaving college forever. Now what? I had been too focused on surviving the Corps to think about how it would feel to leave it.

Hard on the heels of that thought, the fears that had lurked beneath the surface all morning suddenly rose to consciousness. What would happen when I walked across that stage? Would it be the Ring Ceremony all over again? Would there be booing? Hissing? I desperately wanted the school to shine in this final moment; I wanted my graduation to honor my father's school, which was now my own. That is the paradox that every member of the long gray line knows: Every day at The Citadel is a bad day, yet every day is one that you will treasure until the end of your life. In spite of all the pain, I loved this place fiercely. I did not want to see it disgraced in the eyes of the nation. I remembered the media circus that had followed the Shannon Faulkner disaster four years earlier, the horrible publicity of the M&M fiasco my freshman year. "Please God," I prayed, "don't let my graduation become a part of that."

By the time I emerged from under the bleachers and stood ready to climb the steps to the stage, my hands were shaking uncontrollably. The cadet next to me asked me if I was all right. He told me I had turned deathly white, but in my well-hewed style I assured him I was fine. Taking a deep breath, I summoned up three years' worth of courage, and started up the steps.

The moment I saw my father's face, I knew that everything would be all right. I heard the announcer's voice ring out: "Nancy Ruth Mace,

Bachelor of Science in Business Administration, *Magna Cum Laude* Graduate." I heard shouts of congratulation from my family and friends as every dignitary on the stage rose to their feet, among cheers from the audience, and gave me a standing ovation. If anyone hissed, it was drowned out by the applause all around me. Relief flooded my body, and as I reached to shake my father's hand and he handed me my diploma, I saw tears of pride fill his eyes. I had never seen my father cry. Grasping that precious piece of paper, I stepped into my father's arms, and in that single instant, every pain I had endured for three years melted away. I had waited a lifetime to see that look on his face. I had finally made him proud of me, and nothing else really mattered. A moment later, I released him and made my way slowly across the stage, shaking hands with the row of dignitaries still standing in my honor. When I had shaken the very last hand, I turned to the assembled guests and waved my diploma over my head in sheer exuberance. Only when I started down the steps toward my seat did they sit down.

I was heady with relief and awash with emotion. I didn't even mind when the other cadets, few of whom had joined in the cheering for me, rose to give the senior after me a standing ovation of his own. It was a petty gesture, but one I understood. They were reminding me that everyone there should be congratulated, that every graduating cadet deserved to be recognized, that I was nothing special. Well, I had no argument with that. I was part of a brotherhood now and we had all worked hard—harder than we'd ever worked for anything in our lives.

Minutes later we all tossed our covers in the air, and I followed my classmates down the row and toward the exit from McAllister Fieldhouse. The audience was still cheering. As I passed Band Company, playing the recessional that accompanied the graduates out the door, Major Day leaned toward me and held out something. It was his conductor's wand. I looked up at his tall, handsome form, beaming with pride, and I felt a rush of warmth. Three years earlier, this man had told me he regretted the Corps' admission of women. The night before, he had told me that The Citadel was a better place because I had come there. Still smiling, he gestured toward my company mates. I reached out and took the wand from his hand. Stepping up to assume his place, I performed my last act as a Citadel cadet. It was then that I led my company in a final song. They had never sounded better.

★ ★ ★ ★ ★ ★ ★ ★ ★ ★

APPENDIX

PERSONAL MEMORABILIA

AND CORRESPONDENCE

FROM THE CITADEL YEARS

★ ★ ★ ★ ★ ★ ★ ★ ★ ★

The Citadel
The Military College of South Carolina
171 Moultrie Street
Charleston, SC 29409

The Citadel is a comprehensive. liberal arts college within a military environment.

Brief... Very Brief...History

In December 1842, the South Carolina Legislature passed an act establishing a college at the state arsenal at what is known as Marion Square in downtown Charleston. The state militia guards were replaced by 20 young men--the first South Carolina Corps of Cadets. Living under strict discipline the new cadets served as guards for the state's arms while pursuing a course of study designed to educate them to be citizens in peace as well as war.

In 1918 the city gave to the state 100 acres of high ground and salt marsh on the Ashley River near Hampton Park to build an even "Greater Citadel," and in 1922 the college moved to its current location. The coeducational College of Graduate and Professional Studies was founded in 1966 and graduate degree programs were added two years later.

In response to a decision of the United States Supreme Court on June 26, 1996, the Board of Visitors two days later voted unanimously to drop the gender requirement from its admissions policy for Corps of Cadets and the college immediately began accepting women into that program.

Two Diverse, But Equally Important Goals

....To graduate young men and women with alert minds and sound bodies who have been taught the high ideals of honor. integrity, loyalty and patriotism; who accept the responsibilities that accompany leadership; and who have sufficient professional knowledge to take their places in a competitive world. This is accomplished in a unique adversarial and holistic environment, extending beyond that found at other colleges and universities.

...To serve the citizens of the Lowcountry and the state of South Carolina through its coeducational Summer School and College of Graduate and Professional Studies. These programs serve as benchmarks to enrich diversity of The Citadel as an Academic institution.

Facts That May Surprise You

U.S. News & World Report lists The Citadel in the magazine's annual surveys of "America's Best Colleges" and America's Best Values."

In 1995 The Citadel was cited by the Southern Conference for an 88 percent graduation rate of all of our athletes during the previous five-year period was presented the Southern Conference Graduation rate trophy. According to the NCAA, our white and African-American football players who entered in 1988 graduated at the same rate --92 percent--during a six-year period. These statistics are among the very best in the country.

❑ The South Carolina Corps of Cadets is composed of 1.800 young men and women from around the world. Women enrolled in the College of Graduate and Professional studies (CGPS) outnumber the men enrolled in the Corps. ❑ Cadets choose from 20 baccalaureate degree programs. The ratio of students to faculty is approximately 16/1. ❑ The CGPA provides baccalaureate, graduate and doctoral of education degree programs, as well as a broad range of noninstructional activities and services. ❑ Cadets complete eight semesters of Air Force. Army, Navy or Marine Corps ROTC. but they accept a commission only if they are under ROTC contract or hold an ROTC scholarship. About 30 percent of each graduating class enters the military. ❑ There are 84 student interests groups, two national service fraternities, 14 intercollegiate team sports, 19 club sports and 32 intramural programs. Students in the CGPS serve on college-wide committees and councils, and they participate in activities and in student associations. ❑ The 1992 Football Team won the Southern Conference title and ended its regular season ranked #1 in the nation. The 1999, 1995, 1994 and 1990 Baseball Teams won the Southern Conference Championships. The 1990 Bulldogs competed in the World Series, finishing the season ranked #6 in the nation. ❑ The Corps of Cadets, the CGPS and Summer School are supplemented with state appropriations amounting to 27.5 percent of the annual budget..

When to come

The campus is open to visitors from 8a.m. to 6 p.m. daily.
During the college year.....
    the South Carolina Corps of Cadets presents a dress parade on Summerall Field at 3:45 almost every Friday afternoon:
    the Gift Shop is open Monday through Saturday: and
    the Museum is open from 2 to 5 p.m. on Saturday
When the Corps of Cadets is present.....
    Summerall Chapel and Munnerlyn Snack Bar are open daily.

★★★★

★ Upon entering The Citadel, incoming cadet Nancy Mace was given a brief "fast fact" sheet detailing the school's brief history, campus goals, and trivia.

★ 214 ★

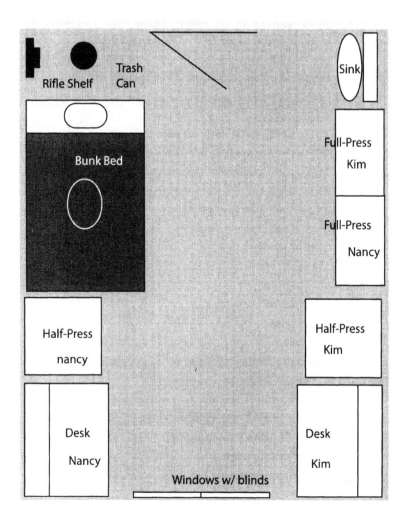

Rifle Shelf Trash Can

Sink

Bunk Bed

Full-Press Kim

Full-Press Nancy

Half-Press nancy

Half-Press Kim

Desk Nancy

Desk Kim

Windows w/ blinds

★ A standard cadet room diagram detailing assigned bunks, desks, and closets for cadets Mace and Messer.

CITADEL FAMILY ASSOCIATION

CITADEL KNOB'S LIST OF MOST NEEDED ITEMS

(SUGGESTED ONLY, BUT RECOMMENDED HIGHLY BY PREVIOUS "KNOB MOMS")

1. SKIN SO SOFT (AVON) TO KEEP GNATS AND NO-SEE-UMS AWAY

2. NAIL POLISH REMOVER (LARGE) FOR REMOVING LACQUER ON BRASS

3. LARGE CAN OF BRASSO (SCHOOL WILL PROVIDE SMALL CAN)

4. BAR KEEPERS FRIEND (FOR POLISHING BRASS; FOUND IN THE GROCERY STORE)

5. TWO (2) LARGE CANS BLACK SHOE POLISH

6. TWO (2) BOTTLES OF SHOE SOLE DRESSING

7. ONE (1) CAN OF PLEDGE OR ENDUST

8. TRAVEL SEWING KIT

9. ASSORTED SAFETY PINS

10. SMALL FLASHLIGHT AND BATTERIES

11. ROLL OF 3/4" MASKING TAPE

12. EXTENSION CORD

13. A THREE OUTLET PLUG STRIP (ESPECIALLY IF YOUR SON HAS A COMPUTER)

14. PENCILS, PENS, STAPLES, STAPLER, PAPER CLIPS

15. EXTRA BLACK COTTON SOCKS (THE HEAVIER CREW-TYPE SOCKS ARE BEST)

16. OLD FLAT WHITE SHEETS TO MAKE BANNERS (MAKE SURE ALL SHEETS ARE FLAT)

17. BLISTER TREATMENT (NU-SKIN OR SECOND SKIN)

18. BAND-AIDS AND FIRST AID CREAM

19. ONE OR TWO OLD TOOTHBRUSHES FOR CLEANING

20. A FEW OLD RAGS FOR POLISHING BRASS AND SHOES

NOTE:
THE SCHOOL WILL SUPPLY SMALL QUANTITIES OF MANY OF THESE ITEMS, BUT IT IS LESS EXPENSIVE TO BUY REFILLS AND REPLACEMENTS AT HOME.

★ A knob's lifesaving list of "must haves" created by former Citadel moms to assist in the adjustment to cadet life.

T·H·E C·I·T·A·D·E·L
THE MILITARY COLLEGE OF SOUTH CAROLINA
CHARLESTON, S.C. 29409

Office of
The Commandant

12 July 1996

INSTRUCTION SHEET

1. Processing will start as early as 0730 and the activities for new cadets will begin at 1300 hrs (1:00 PM), Saturday, 24 August. It is to your advantage to arrive during the morning hours to expedite your initial processing.

2. Enclosed with these instructions is a card marked with the letter of the company to which you have been assigned. Place this in the middle of your car's windshield (or have the taxi driver do so if you have come to Charleston via commercial transportation). This card will enable the cadet traffic detail to direct you to the proper barracks. You should enter The Citadel campus by Lesesne Gate (Main Gate) at the West end of Moultrie Street.

3. When you reach your barracks, a cadet guard will direct you to a parking area. You should unload your baggage, place it in a designated area, and report to your company's Cadet First Sergeant who will be seated inside the Sallyport (ENTRANCE) of your barracks. He will give you your room assignment. At this time, you should take your baggage to your room. If your father or any other male friend is with you, he may help you take your baggage to your room. After that, you should return to your First Sergeant to begin processing, and your father or friend is then asked to leave the barracks.

4. Should you arrive at The Citadel prior to Saturday, 24 August, please inform the guard at Lesesne Gate that you are an incoming Fourth Classman and give him the designation of the company to which you have been assigned. Ask the guard to direct you to the appropriate barracks. Report to the barracks **guardroom**, located in the **East Sallyport** (ENTRANCE) of the appropriate barracks. A member of the cadet guard will direct you to the room to which you have been assigned. Then move your luggage into your room. The guard will also inform you of the time and place for your meals. At 1300, 24 August, you are to report to your Cadet First Sergeant, as discussed in paragraph 3 of this letter.

★ To avoid confusion on the first day of orientation, the above instructions are sent to entering cadets regarding the processing procedure.

FRESHMAN REPORTING DATE
SATURDAY
AUGUST 24, 1996

The Class of 2000 will report no later than 1:00 p.m. on Saturday, August 24, 1996. The barracks will open to receive freshmen at 10:00 a.m. Early arrival is recommended.

Freshmen and their families should plan for lunch on their own. The evening meal will be the first provided for freshmen by The Citadel.

ACADEMIC ORIENTATION

An *Academic Orientation* will be conducted on Saturday, August 24, and Sunday, August 25. The orientation will occur before military training begins and is designed to introduce freshmen to the academic environment of the college. Additional information regarding the orientation will be sent during the summer.

Military training will begin on Monday, 26 August.

THE CITADEL'S FOURTH CLASS SYSTEM

The purpose of The Citadel's Fourth Class System is to develop and graduate the "whole man."

The Citadel System is the completeness with which it matures, refines, trains and schools the totality of a young man's character. This finely balanced process is called the "whole man" concept. During four years, cadets will be developed academically, physically, militarily and spiritually.

These personal qualities must be deeply ingrained in the individual so that neither time nor dilemmas will diminish his respect for complying with the customs and traditions set forth for the fourthclassman's conduct. The traditions of The Citadel cannot be maintained by men who will do no more than is required of them. Self-discipline and self-evaluation develop men whose integrity and sense of duty cause them to serve selflessly beyond the prescribed limits of their tasks.

The Fourth Class System is both difficult and demanding. It represents an abrupt change from the life normally experienced in the home and encompasses the entire period of a cadet's first year at The Citadel. It is administered impersonally but at the same time exhibits the individual understanding necessary for effective leadership. It requires a full measure of mental preparedness and physical endurance.

★ A brief explanation of cadet orientation and the "fourth class system."

SECOND BATTALION HEADQUARTERS
THE MILITARY COLLEGE OF SOUTH CAROLINA
THE CITADEL

MEMORANDUM   **24 AUGUST 1996**
ACADEMIC ORIENTATION RULES

To: Incoming knobs
From: Second Battalion Academic Officer
Subject: Battalion life policy during academic orientation

1. Use of vending machines prohibited

2. Knobs must stay in his/her own room except for use of the bathroom

3. No talking in the galleries

4. No congregating on galleries

5. Use of pay phones prohibited

6. Knobs must be in full PT's at all times

7. Knobs are only allowed to address upperclassmen on academic staff

---

★ General rules governing knobs of the 2nd Battalion during academic orientation. These rules would have to be observed for X weeks.

THE CADET 24 HOUR SCHEDULE

A.   General.   The Cadet 24 Hour Schedule is a key ingredient of the
environment which contributes to the intense, high stress nature of the fourth
class system.   The 24 Hour Schedule also provides structure and formality to
every aspect of cadet life.   Familiarity with the schedule, and conduct of
daily activities within the parameters established by the schedule, become
second nature to all cadets shortly after arrival.

B.   The Cadet 24 Hour Schedule and Schedule of Bugle calls is as follows:

CADET 24-HOUR SCHEDULE

WEEKDAYS
Monday thru Thursday

0530		Barracks Gate Open
0600	*	First Call, Fourth Class Cadets on Line
0602	*	Steele - Fourth Class Cadets Onto Quad
0605	*	Unit Physical Training (PT)
0645	*	Steele - End PT
0645-0710	*	Personal Hygiene
0700-0745		Sick Call
0710		Mess Call, Fourth Class Cadets on Line
0712		Steele - Fourth Class Cadets Move Onto Quad
0715		Assembly/Reveille/March to Breakfast
0720		Breakfast
0735		Announcements/Second Rest
0750		Class Call
0800-1150		Classes, MSP and MRI
1100	**	First Call - Drill, Fourth Class Cadets on Line
1102	**	Steele - Fourth Class Cadets Onto Quad
1105	**	Assembly - Drill
1205		Mess Call, Fourth Class Cadets on Line
1207		Steele - Fourth Class Cadets Move Onto Quad
1210		Assembly, Inspection, March to Lunch
1220		Lunch
1235		Announcements/Second Rest
1250		Class Call
1300-1450		Afternoon Class, ASP (Certain Labs until 1650)
1500-1800	***	Tours and Confinements
1530-1730		Intramurals,
1715		Guard Mount - Assembly
1810		First Call, Retreat, Fourth Class Cadets on Line
1812		Steele, Fourth Class Cadets Move Onto Quad
1815		Assembly, Retreat
1820		March to Supper
1825		Supper
1840		Announcements/Second Rest
1840-1930		Cadets who will not be in the Barracks at 1930 must sign out.
1840-1930		Company Admin time
1930		ESP begins - All In taken.
2130		Cadets may go to bed, and no Fourth Class Cadets Visitation.
2230-2300		Commanders are authorized to conduct limited administration. These activities will not cause a disturbance of ESP or involve Fourth Class Cadets.
2300		Taps, All Cadets must be in the Barracks, All in Check
2400	****	Fourth Class Cadets lights out, the period of ESP ends
0100	****	Upperclass Cadets lights out, the period of ESP ends

* Tuesdays and Thursdays, Unit PT; Mondays, Wednesdays
   and Fridays, ROTC PT as required
** Tuesdays and Thursdays
*** Wednesdays
**** Only Cadets with authorized Late Light Pass
   displayed on their door are permitted Late Lights
   beyond 2400/0100.

★ Required to adhere to a very precise schedule in their first year, entering cadets are sent this sample twenty-four-hour schedule for reference.

★ 220 ★

NOTES: (1)   Cadet Activity meetings may be held at 1840 hrs. Monday
through Thursday. All Cadets must be in barracks or other study area for ESP
at 2000 hours.
          (2)   General leave is authorized on Wednesdays (upper 3 classes
only) from after the cadet's last scheduled activity (NET 1200 hrs.) until
1900 hrs. Evening meal optional (Class 1 - 3), retreat formation held at 1920
hrs.

FRIDAY

0530-1500	Same as weekdays (M-Th)
1520	First Call to Parade, Fourth Class Cadets on Line
1522	Steele, Fourth Class Cadets onto Quad
1525	Assembly
1545	Adjutant's Call to Parade
1700	General Leave begins after Parade
1730	Guard Mount - Assembly
1800	Optional Supper
1900-2200	Tours and Confinements
2400	All-ins taken (Fourth Class Cadets)
0100	All-ins taken (Upper Class Cadets)

SATURDAY

TBD	SMI
TBD	Unit PT
0640	Mess Call, Fourth Class Cadets On Line
0642	Steele, Fourth Class Cadets Move Onto Quad
0645	Assembly/Reveille
0650	March to Breakfast
0655	Breakfast
0700-0730	Sick Call
0710	Announcements/Second Rest
1200-2400/0100	General Leave following completion of Military/Cadet Duty
1205	Lunch - Optional
1300-1500	Re-inspection if required
1400-1700	Tours and Confinements
1200-2400	Fourth Class General Leave if released from SMI re-inspection
1200-0100	General Leave for Upperclass if released from SMI re-inspection
1730-1830	Optional Supper
1900-2200	Tours and Confinements
2300	Taps
2400	Fourth Class Cadets All In
0100	Upperclass All In

NOTE: Saturday morning will normally include an SMI, Unit PT/CPFT and/or
Unit Training: Times To Be Determined

SUNDAY

0835	Church Call
0900	Chapel Services (Protestant)
1000-1300	Optional Brunch
1700-1750	Optional Supper
1710	First Call - Guard Mount
1715	Guard Mount
1800	End of General Leave for Fourth Class Cadets
1830	End of General Leave for Upper Class Cadets
1845	First Call - Fourth Class Cadets on Line
1847	Steele, Fourth Class Cadets onto Quad
1850	Retreat
1900	Chapel Services (Catholic/Protestant)
1930	ESP begins- All-in taken
2130	Cadets may go to bed, and no Fourth Class Cadets Visitation
2230-2300	Commanders are authorized to conduct limited administration. These activities will not cause a distrubance of ESP or involve Fourth Class Cadets.
2300	Taps, All cadets must be in the Barracks, All-in Check
2400	*** Lights out for Fourth Class Cadets
0100	*** Lights out for Upperclass Cadets

     *** Only Cadets with authorized Late Light passes displayed on their
door are permitted Late Light beyond 2400/0100.

9/25/96

Dearest Mom and Dad,

How are things going? I have some time at the moment and I wanted to write you two a very straightforward letter. All the other times I have written or called I have been quick and dirty, but now I really want to spend time in this letter.

At the moment I have a cold and do not feel 100% well, but I am keeping up to task just fine. We have to run the laundry in a little while, what fun, I hope I do not get anyone from the Regimental Staff. (I would have to go up to the top level, drive stairs and be in an environment that I am not accustomed to—). Anyway, I am kind of tired. I think it's terrible that we cannot turn our lights out until 2230. I have had some problems thus far with my roommate, but as each day turns over I pray things will get better and we can understand each other. I try to make an effort to make things happen around here, but it is really hard for me when I know we have major differences not only in our behavior, but attitude and goals as well. I hope to be sending along to you guys some of the letters I get from people, I especially want you to see the two official statements I have written this week. Someone has gotten into trouble (an upperclassman). I won't go into detail about that, but I will say I have not been harmed in any way. Mr. Thaxton, my CO, said I did an outstanding job on them, I typed them up and put them in an envelope. My letters were so professional, it was cool.

I am still receiving mail from people I don't even know, from all different places too. I am sending out my letters concerning my ADD to most all of my professors this week. So, there is no need to worry about that. I got my first A on a test today, I was thrilled, I had no idea, although yesterday I bombed an English quiz and I could feel the light tears watering my eyes. I think my professor

★ One of the first and more-detailed letters Nancy sent home after arriving at school in the summer of 1996 outlines the many frustrations she experienced as a fourth class cadet.

noticed I was not happy because he asked me if I was all right. And now, I am.

I feel far away from you guys even though the drive there is only twenty-five to thirty minutes. It is tough on all of us four girls, but I feel it is tougher on me because I am the only female in my company. I am, however, pleased with my overall performance, I hope you guys are too. I have yet to drop from a PT run, unlike some of my fellow male classmates. My grades aren't half that bad, although there is much room for improvement, I am not up to my academic standards, but will be very soon I hope. Have there been many calls from old friends still? Are you surprised that I have stuck this long? Like Dad said, "I am not going to let these SOB's run me out." No way, no how.

I feel far away from you guys, and distant. I guess because this big decision of mine was pretty swift. Do you feel the same way? I know you guys love me and care about me, but why does it feel so distant? Sometimes I feel like you aren't thinking about me. Is it because I don't see a lot of y'all or talk to y'all? Maybe, but still. I have no idea what on earth your lives are like at this moment. I have no idea how Dad is doing with his new job, I have no idea for how long he is going to be in Columbia. I have no idea what his status in this new job is. I haven't gotten any mail from James and only one note from Dad. Why? Are you guys that busy? I am under a hell of a lot of pressure and I get lonely. It is hard for me to bond with everyone down here, half the guys in my squad are either wusses or think they know it all. . . . And the other three girls are doing their own thing, and here I am stuck in a small cell alone. Do you have any idea of this pressure? I have written to James many times and I have yet to get a response, is he alive and well? See, I have no clue as to what your lives are like. Mom, how are your classes going? James, how are your classes going? Dad, are you enjoying your time with the new job? Are my cat and dog friends doing fine without me? Call me homesick, I think I am just lonely and disappointed because I have no idea what on earth is going on with you all. I hardly ever get to talk to you guys and you're family. Yeah, I get one little e-line that says hello, but where is the rest? I spend a lot of my time by myself. It is tough, but I am doing it.

On most mornings before morning formation, I arrive at room 2154 to pick up two of my classmates, well they are not usually ready, then I spend at least another five minutes with them. Then we go to pick up the rest in our squad room, and they have yet to be ready when the rest of us are—this is [A] and [B]. They make me sick, then there is [C] and [D], always take their time. When we get to the final destination in 2135 our "real" squad room we are by that time late. I get so ticked off like you wouldn't believe. The first two guys I pick up sometimes make me mad. [E] is moody and snotty, and both he and his roommate think they know it all. We try to hold meetings, but I just sit there and analyze it the whole time and think to myself you have to be kidding me. It is really not this bad, but this week has been terrible. [A] and [B] and some of the others I have mentioned have gotten us into some type of trouble. I admit, I am not perfect by any means, but you know how it is, I like to be prompt. Even if my shirt-tuck looks nasty. [F] always goes out the door first, he will even jump in front of me to get out the door first, I am like, "Hold up, I can do this too." Like if he is first he is better than all of us. Anyway. My classmates don't know how they tick me off so much. Just little things. I think some of the cadre is trying us. I am ready to turn on some of these weak boys. Some don't even care like [B] and [A]. They make me sick because they are so slow. Like this evening, we were given an order to form up outside our staff sergeant's door immediately following supper, well, all of us were there and ten to fifteen minutes later (still bracing, sweating, and screaming) the cadre finds our classmate [B] sitting in his room without the light on. I guess he was hiding out. (And he is transferring from the merchant marines.) I wanted to yell at him so badly. I am sorry you have to listen to this, but I don't have anyone else to tell. Then, another thing is that since I am basically living in this room alone, I have no idea about what the schedule is. Did I tell you guys that my squad left me Saturday morning? They didn't see me before formation and they didn't come wake me up. I always get there early and if I am not there something is wrong. I don't know, I guess we are all broken.

I am sorry you had to hear that, it really isn't that bad, just some ignorance of my classmates. I can't tell you how many times during sweep detail [A] or somebody has wiped out my shoes because they weren't paying attention, and [B] is just plain slow. No purpose whatsoever. Anyway, I am going to get off this subject, it really isn't this bad, we have just had a pretty stressful week I guess. And, we need to start bonding together and holding our own shine parties and whatnot.

Anyway, I hope I didn't tick anyone off. I heard there was still a guard outside the knobs door (the guy who was on "48 Hours"). I got barked at today by an officer in Echo, he was the knob they portrayed on "48 Hours" in May. He is mean. He said I was looking at my watch on his galleries, well that is false, but I took the heat anyway. He should be grateful I didn't accidentally blow him off. I did that yesterday to a group of guys from Echo. I didn't mean to. Oh well, maybe they have forgotten. I passed someone in Bond Hall this evening and he told me I did a good job on the other night on "48 Hours". Do you have a copy of the tape? Kim has seen it and I am kind of curious. I hope there hasn't been a bunch of media bothering you guys. I have gotten letters saying that people want the rights to my story. Trust me, that thought did not stay in my mind for more than a miniature millisecond. I kept the letter so you could read it sometime. I'd like to come home this weekend or next. Just to relax and sleep. I invited James to the first hop—has he mentioned it to you? If not, ask him. I think it would be fun to take my brother. I think some of the other girls are taking their brothers. Anyway, I think he might enjoy it. I need to go, I have to start studying. I am getting an A on my test in Health tomorrow, and we also have a paper to turn in with it, and I finished that on Tuesday.

Love ya,
Please keep in touch
NR

From: MACEN@Citadel.edu
Date sent: Sun, 13 Oct 1996 18:59:15 -0400 (EDT)
Subject: For Dad
To: amace@awod.com

Dear Dad,

Thank you for coming to see me this weekend; I enjoyed our time together although I wish it were longer. I was excited that you were able to see my room. You do not know what a thrill it was when I found out that you saw your old room, I think that is awesome. When I find myself pondering the question of "why" I came here I think about you, your life accomplishments, and your life here at The Citadel. I never in my wildest dream believed I would be here at this school. It still is hard to imagine that I am walking in your path, doing the same activities that you did in college. There are times when I think I hate it here, but when I am in parades, at the games, and outside the gate, I almost want to love the place.

I like to think a lot when I have the time. I cannot get over the fact that I am in the same barracks that you lived in. When I do sweep details I think about you doing the same sweep details, it almost brings tears to my eyes and has a few times already because like I said earlier, I am walking in your steps to a life that will hopefully be as successful as yours IS.

I hope you and mom and James enjoyed the parade. For the first time I didn't make any drastic mistakes, just a few minor ones that hopefully no one noticed. I am actually playing the songs although when the beat

---

★ Nancy communicated mostly through e-mail to her parents and siblings. This letter to her father (before he joined The Citadel staff) was one of many that expressed her excitement, trepidation, and pride in attending her father's alma mater.

picks up and the notes are faster I have a difficult time keeping up, I will admit that. I had a great breakfast this morning. I can't remember the last time I laughed that hard. Thanks. We joke around here as much as possible, but there really isn't enough time for all that. I am glad that I could entertain you with those stories I know there will be more to come.

Do you have any good ideas or hints or tips on survival for the next seven and a half months? I hide a well-ironed shirt behind my desk, I plan to get one of those flat, no-noise vacuums to put under my half-press (they don't make any noise, they are usually used in restaurants and some of my classmates have them). Plus, I heard we have an SMI on the weekend of October 26. That is what I heard from Maj. Powell over in Admissions.

What sort of stuff do you hear about me? I am sure it is all good, although our company upperclass thinks we are the worst knobs to have entered the school's history.

Well, I need to be going, I have a review session for my accounting test tomorrow—I plan to do my best.

These next few weeks are going to be tough, but I am going to try my hardest. I will be in touch, I will be strong, and I will be thinking of you and the rest of the family as always. I was stopped today before entering the barracks and the JOD asked me if I prayed a lot. Well, I told him yes, but do you know what his answer was? He said, "Well, that's good because that's the only thing that will get you through this week." I didn't know whether to laugh, cry, or stick it to him, so I went to my room. Wish me luck; I will need it during this next week or two.

Love you guys a lot,
NR

Not only do we "bitches" pay taxes to support the Citadel but also to support your own life of ease... Your daughter is - getting a free ride into The Citadel after no legal expense on her parents' part to make this education available to all capable women.

"the Citadel man's deep contempt for "females," or "whales" or "bitches"

How low can you go?

★ Throughout Nancy's attendance at The Citadel, the Mace family received numerous letters from outraged cadets, their parents, alumni, and local residents. This letter was sent to Nancy's mother during the first few months of Nancy's enrollment.

From: MACEN@Citadel.edu
Date sent: Mon, 16 Dec 1996 14:17:46 -0400 (EDT)
Subject: two babies
To: amace@awod.com

Did you know which two cadets are on campus, in civvies? Guess. I am sure it is a real hard question. I am hanging in Bond Hall because I can't quite make it to the library; there are cameras by Lesegne Gate. I don't feel like being on TV today, sorry channel four. :(. They got their parents to ask for "special permission" for them to reside off campus with their families and take exams, possibly off campus too. A bunch of you know what's, wusses. *Whah whah whah*, I wanta go home, *whah whah whah*. I am surprised they haven't withdrawn yet. Do you guys know anything I don't? I heard they haven't quit yet. Why not? They opted to cheese out of the exams and campus life. They are bags looking for excuses to leave. Well, all and total respect lost for them and their families. It is sad, and I feel for the Mentavlos family because they did have a lot of respect, but they have been losing their glow for some time now, with Jeanie's behavior. If they come back into the corps next semester, I don't see how they could stand to stay, unless the justice department takes away the fourth class system. You know they are going to be shunned. No one is allowed to talk to them if they see them on campus. I heard they were chilling out on campus today in civvies, and prettying themselves up.

Anti-knobs, ex-knob, ex-cadet with no respect.
I am going to assist the dean of recruitment by signing and editing a letter to be sent out to applicants, mainly women. He is going to put the main gist of the letter together for me by Wednesday, and I will pick it

---

★ After filing charges, cadets Messner and Mentavlos finally leave campus, and Nancy is even more determined to finish what she started. This e-mail was written shortly before Nancy and Petra take the cadet oath and leave the fourth class system behind.

up and edit it and fill in the blanks as I see fit. Can't wait. When he brought it up among the faculty that one of the four should help write the letter, my name was unanimously picked. Kind of cool, right? Petra and I are supposed to stay together because the rules say that no female is allowed to stay alone. Well, I wish I had known that so that I could have pulled Kim. I might if she comes back. There is no way that Petra or I could room with either one of them, and the administration is doing their hardest to find a way to get us together next semester if "frick and frack" come back. But if one leaves then two need to leave because I refuse to live in an alcove because I am not an upperclassman and do not deserve that privilege.

We are getting an alarm button put in both rooms that will signal the guard, and Saturday night we both received cellular phones, just in case. In my own personal opinion I think the school is watching their back with the Justice Department, which is fine. I, however, do not feel threatened. Today, double-timing it to formation, I could hear "Mace, one of the last few," "drive on hard charger," "locked-on," "put out Mace," and in the Mess Hall after General Poole's address, a knob said to my rear "never quit, right Mace?" My only reply was "NEVER." I almost had tears in my eyes. Today on campus an upperclassman casually passes by, "rock out, you hear me?" You don't know how good it felt. I am sure there were a few silent cadets, who are probably more disgusted with women, but I can't help that and they know P and I are trying our hardest. Col. Legare just came to the window with a thumbs-up. I have received e-mail from people wishing me the best and to stay focused. But what meant the most today were the solemn whispers and coaches by upperclassmen from other companies. I nearly wanted to cry when I heard their voices. Driving by Hotel, a dreaded company, they stared sadly and told me to "drive on." You don't know how good it felt.

I am floating on a cloud even though I am mentally exhausted. The respect we have is sincerely tremendous and I could see it today. Classmates giving P and I pats on the back with their concern and mail. One knob e-mailed me just to tell me that he heard that P and I are locked on and were quitting. I of course thanked him and said that "quit" was not in our vocabulary. I just want to collapse, but I must move on and focus on what is important—exams. Although, it will be difficult, I will give it my best and pray. I will pray that everything will work out, and it will, no matter how my finals turn out, I have made it halfway through the most difficult challenge in my life thus far. I am proud to be a Citadel Cadet and with most especially a knob. I will miss this fourth-class year when it is all over with.

I hope both you and Dad realize the amount of love I have for this institution even though I have broken the ice with a long-standing tradition. Whether or not everyone wants us women to stay, their opinions have no more effect on my decisions. I have finally accepted the fact that I cannot change everyone, so I must hold my head high and look straightforward. But in the end, this school will give me character and make me a stronger person, just like you and Dad. Take care, and pray we do our best each and every day.

Love to all,
Nancy

H. 4130.

Introduced by Representatives Lee, Allison, Cobb-Hunter, Gamble, Gilham, Hinson, Martin, Meacham, Miller, Moody-Lawrence, Neilson, Parks, Rodgers, Seithel, Stuart and Young-Brickell.

A CONCURRENT RESOLUTION

TO COMMEND NANCY RUTH MACE OF GOOSE CREEK FOR HER LEADERSHIP, EXEMPLARY CONDUCT, AND OUTSTANDING ACHIEVEMENTS WHILE A CADET AT THE CITADEL, THE MILITARY COLLEGE OF SOUTH CAROLINA; TO CONGRATULATE NANCY RUTH MACE ON BECOMING THE FIRST FEMALE CADET TO GRADUATE FROM THE CITADEL AND FOR GRADUATING MAGNA CUM LAUDE; TO RECOGNIZE NANCY RUTH MACE AS THE CADET WHO SET THE STANDARD TO BE EMULATED BY ALL OTHER FEMALES WHO BECOME MEMBERS OF THE SOUTH CAROLINA CORPS OF CADETS; AND TO FURTHER RECOGNIZE NANCY RUTH MACE AS THE PROTOTYPE OF THE CITADEL WOMAN, AND A GENUINE SOURCE OF PRIDE TO HER ALMA MATER, TO SOUTH CAROLINA, AND TO WOMEN EVERYWHERE, AS SHE TAKES HER PLACE IN THE CITADEL'S DISTINGUISHED LONG GRAY LINE AS THE FIRST FEMALE CADET TO GRADUATE FROM THIS WORLD RENOWNED MILITARY COLLEGE.

WHEREAS, a new day has dawned at The Citadel, The Military College of South Carolina, with the graduation on Saturday, May 8, 1999, of Nancy Ruth Mace, the first female cadet to graduate from the once all-male distinguished military college; and

WHEREAS, Nancy Ruth Mace was born December 4, 1977, at Ft. Bragg, North Carolina, the daughter of Frances Anne Jamison Mace, Ed.D., and Brigadier General James Emory Mace, Sr., United States Army, Retired, a 1963 graduate of The Citadel and the current Commandant of Cadets; and

WHEREAS, Nancy Ruth Mace graduated from Stratford High School in Charleston in 1995, and spent the following year at a local community college. An outstanding student and fine athlete, Nancy Ruth Mace was by qualifications, instinct, and inclination a natural candidate for the rigors of life in the barracks as a cadet and member of the South Carolina Corps of Cadets. In August of 1996, Nancy Ruth Mace was one of four women who got her hair cut, donned cadet gray, joined her classmates as a "knob" in Band Company, and took her place in ranks as a member of the South Carolina Corps of Cadets who came to stay; and

---

★ Upon Nancy's graduation from the "Corps of Cadets" as the first female graduate, the South Carolina General Assembly honors her with a resolution of outstanding achievement.

WHEREAS, since June 28, 1996, when the Board of Visitors unanimously voted to admit women into the Corps, female cadets have become an increasing presence at The Citadel. The success of Cadet Nancy Ruth Mace proved inspirational to many other young women who aspired to attend The Citadel. Throughout the recruiting of qualified females by The Citadel, Cadet Mace was an asset in the college's efforts to assimilate women into the classroom, the barracks, and as full-fledged members of the Corps of Cadets; and

WHEREAS, as a cadet Nancy Ruth Mace excelled academically, graduating magna cum laude, with a cumulative grade point average of 3.678 and a 3.8 in her major, for which she was inducted into the business honor society. She was a member of Band Company and made an invaluable contribution to the Regimental Band as a musician. She was selected after her plebe year to serve on the cadre as a cadet corporal, training the next year's incoming freshmen. She represented The Citadel as a member of the color guard at the opening cadet at The Citadel, Nancy Ruth Mace set the standard for all other female cadets at The Citadel to emulate. The first female cadet to graduate from The Citadel, she is the first female cadet proto-graduate and the prototype of the Citadel woman. She is a source of pride to her parents, to her alma mater, to South Carolina, and to women everywhere.

NOW, THEREFORE,

BE IT RESOLVED by the House of Representatives, the Senate concurring:

THAT the members of the General Assembly of the State of South Carolina, by this resolution, hereby commend Nancy Ruth Mace of Goose Creek for her leadership, exemplary conduct, and outstanding achievements while a cadet at The Citadel, The Military College of South Carolina; congratulate Nancy Ruth Mace on becoming the first female cadet to graduate from The Citadel and for graduating magna cum laude; recognize Nancy Ruth Mace as the female cadet who set the standard to be emulated by all other females who become members of the South Carolina Corps of Cadets at The Citadel; and further recognize Nancy Ruth Mace as the prototype of The Citadel woman and a genuine source of pride to her alma mater, to South Carolina, and to women everywhere, as she takes her place in The Citadel's distinguished long gray line and as the first female cadet to graduate from this world renowned military college.

BE IT FURTHER RESOLVED that a copy of this resolution be presented to Nancy Ruth Mace of Goose Creek.

State of South Carolina
In the House of Representatives
Columbia, South Carolina
May 19, 1999

We hereby certify that the foregoing is a true and correct copy of a resolution passed in the House of Representatives and concurred in by the Senate.

David H. Wilkins
Speaker

Sandra K. McKinney
Clerk of the House

★ PHOTO CREDITS ★

★ ACKNOWLEDGMENTS ★

There are many individuals who have provided solace and support throughout my experience at The Citadel. I must thank each and every one of you who have, at some point, been a pillar in my life.

First, I extend my sincerest gratitude toward Simon & Schuster for providing the opportunity to tell this story. Moreover, I would like to acknowledge Amy-Hampton Knight, my editor; Mary Jane Ross, my coauthor; and Tandy Rice, my agent.

I want to acknowledge my dearest husband, Christopher, for his unconditional love and devotion, my sisters and their families: Beth, John, Lacey, Will, Harley, and Mace McGrath; Mary, Michael, Jacob, Matthew, and Katie Beth Baumeister; my younger brother, James, who has always been an inspiration for my academic success; my Auntie Beth and Uncle Jimmy; and my two cousins Amy and David Bumgardner. Additional familial support has been provided by Mr. and Mrs. Mac Gardner, Dr. Bill and Dr. Nancy Dabney Hart, the Joe Harvey Family, Mr. and Mrs. Bob Mace, Mr. and Mrs. Mark Niemiec and their children Jessica and Tyler, Mrs. Mildred Niemiec, Mrs. Evelyn Thomas, and Mr. John Thomas.

I am deeply grateful to The Citadel Board of Visitors who made the decision to allow women to enter the gates of The Citadel. This decision not only gave me, but every woman that graduates the opportunity of a lifetime.

I would also like to recognize the efforts of the President of The Citadel Major General John S. Grinalds and his wife. Moreover, I am grateful to the following faculty, staff, and administration: Mrs. Heather Anderson, CSM Sylvan Bauer, Dr. Mark Bebensee, Dr. Nancy Bell, MSG Teresa Blackman, Professor Cynthia Bolt-Lee, Cdr. Barbara Boyd, Col. Floyd Brown (deceased) and his wife, Col. Dennis Carpenter, Maj. Elizabeth Carter, Dr. John Carter, Col. and Mrs. Charles Clanton, Maj. and Mrs. Herb Day, Col. and Mrs. James Dorton, Cpt. Richard Ellis, Col. John Folley, Ms. Kelly Frick, Lt. Col. Hank Fuller, Mrs. Clarietha Gaines, Capt. Rose Gay, Mr. David Heidenberg, Col. Joel Heiser, Lt. Col. Houchen, Mr. Tommy Hunter, Col. Richard Irby, Ms. Geraldine Jones, Maj. and Mrs. Sandy Jones, Mr. Al Katz, Dr. Thomas Kindel, Lt. Col. Steve Klein,

Maj. Jeffrey Koob, Col. John Lackey, Lt. Col. Angie LeClerq, Mrs. Nancy Lefter, Lt. Col. Ben Legare, Capt. Robert Loftin, Dr. Peter Mailloux, Ms. Patricia McArver, Mrs. Vera Mims, Dr. Dorothy Moore, Mr. Gerald Murray, Lt. Col. Herbert Nath, Lt. Cmdr. Drury Nimmich, Maj. Bruce Norton, Dr. Suzanne Ozment, Mr. Russ Pace, BG and Mrs. R. Clifton Poole, Maj. John Powell, Col. George Powers, Capt. Jeffrey Price, Mrs. Susan Redmond, Col. Charles Reger, Capt. Karen Reichardt, Col. James Rembert, Col. John Rivers, Capt. Naomi Russi, Dr. Conway Saylor, Lt. Col. Robert Sberna, Dr. William Sharbrough, Ms. Karen Shuler, Mrs. Carolyn Smalldridge, Maj. Steven Smith, Mr. Louis Spearman, Dr. Christopher Spivey, Ms. Susan Spurlock, Mr. Brent Stewart, Professor Arnold Strauch, Mr. Noel Thorn, Col. Joseph Trez, Col. Donald Tomasik, Ms. Joan Vaughan, Ms. Jennifer Wallace, Cdr. Bruce Williams, Dr. Gary Wilson, and Dr. Barbara Zaremba. Each and every one of them are a part of my journey.

My gratitude is extended to the Long Gray Line especially to the graduates who have been supportive of the coeducation efforts. These individuals include: Mr. Pat Conroy, Mr. Nat Davis, Senator Ernest 'Fritz' Hollings, Mr. Walt Hood, Ambassador Tony Motley, Charleston Mayor Joseph P. Riley, Dr. Henry Rittenburg, Mr. Skip Wharton, and Mr. George McCracken my high school principal and Citadel graduate who saw my potential and recommended me for admission. My appreciation reaches to other cadets and graduates of The Citadel: Dena Abrash, Merv Acevedo, Ryan Bailey, Pete Baltos, Jim Begley, Allyn Brooks-Lasure, Tim Brock, Nate Brooks, James Browning, Frank Bruzzi, Bryant Butler, Phil Buzzetta, Frank Caldwell, Dustin Calhoun, William "Stugie" Carroll, Jennifer Causey, Mark Chandler, Cory Chinn, Matthew Church, Mac Coker, Cecil Collins, Danny Cooper, King Cooper, Deonn Crumley, Ethan Davis, Melanie De Santiago, James Dillahey, Mike Doria, Chris Duncan, Mike Dye, Stephen "Big Bird" Foland, Adam Freeman, Mandy Garcia, Graham Grafton, Rob Graham, David Greer, Rueben Gresham, Eileen Guerra, Nick Hampton, Coburn Hartsell, Rob Hood, Mark Howell, Ben Ingram, Garrett Jackson, Paul Jakubowski, Josh Jenkins, Peter Jennings, Courtney Jones, Ryan Jones, Jay Kaufman, Drew Kelly, Thomas Kennedy, Bryan King, Phil Kiniery, Chris Koehler, John Laurel, Petra Lovetinska, Morgan Lynn, Steve Markey, Mark McAfee, Dave Maher, Tom McAlister, Mike McKee, Lee Miller, Kris Mitchell,

Travis Mooney, Brian Moore, Michael Murphy, Richard Musto, Ryan Nash, John Norris, Christian Pappas, John Parquette, Keith Pereira, Brandy Perry, Delmer Powell, Tony Rausa, David Rawlinson, Evan Reich, Will Riley, Jason Rochester, Adrian Rodzianko, Erik Rudiger, Dave Santos, John Sarto, Noel Sawatzky, Jason Sharp, Chip Shuler, Matt Sino, Patrik Smida, Jerrid Smith, Jason Southern, Alex Sparra, Crystal Spring, Scott Taylor, Steve Thaxton, Mark Thomann, Shawn Tobias, Hank Tolley, Chris Turner, Ted Uppole, Tony Vause, Pete Vorster, Heather Ward, Richard Watts, Joel Wells, Dave Weiner, Jason Wemitt, Reed Wilson, Scott Wizeman, Naz Yangco, and Yancey Zinkon.

I must acknowledge the mentorship provided by the Baker family, Dr. Sharon Balcome, Mrs. Lucy Beckham, Mrs. Susan Davenport, Mrs. Sandy Mallard, Mr. and Mrs. Lem Pendley, Mr. and Mrs. Steve Pendley, Dr. Bill Quesenberry, Coach Tom Schmidt, and Ms. Paulette Walker.

Moreover, I am thankful to The Citadel Development Foundation Scholarship, Class of 1963 Scholarship, The Daniel Fund, Janet Twitty Scholarship, Jesse Ball Dupont Scholarship, and the LIFE Scholarship for the financial support.

Everyone mentioned on these pages has provided inspiration throughout the journey, which led me to and through The Citadel experience. And, I have learned an entire lifetime of lessons with your help; and without each and every one of you I would not be standing where I am today. I am blessed; I will forever be grateful for the sustenance, which has endowed my life with all of the wonderfully unique experiences I had while at The Citadel.

Finally, I want to acknowledge those few individuals who remain adamant in their belief that The Citadel is a far worse place today because there are women among its cadet ranks. All who enter the gates on a hot Saturday in August embark on the "road less traveled" whether male or female. It is a road I am proud to have had the opportunity to take.